DAW
6/57

STALIN'S
INSTRUMENTS
OF TERROR

STALIN'S
INSTRUMENTS
OF TERROR

CHEKA • OGPU • NKVD • KGB
FROM 1917 TO 1991

RUPERT BUTLER

SPELLMOUNT

British Library Cataloguing in Publication Data:
A catalogue record for this book is available
from the British Library

Copyright © Amber Books Ltd 2006

ISBN-13: 978-1-86227-350-4
ISBN-10: 1-86227-350-2

First published in the UK in 2006 by
SPELLMOUNT LTD
The Mill
Brimscombe Port
Stroud
Gloucestershire GL5 3QG

Tel: 01453 883300
Fax: 01453 883233
e-mail: enquiries@spellmount.com
Website: www.spellmount.com

Editorial and design by
Amber Books Ltd
Bradley's Close
74-77 White Lion Street
London N1 9PF
www.amberbooks.co.uk

Project Editor: Michael Spilling
Design: Anthony Cohen
Picture Research: Terry Forshaw

Printed in Dubai

AUTHOR'S ACKNOWLEDGMENTS
The author would particularly like to thank Donald Rayfield, Professor of Russian and Georgian at
Queen Mary College (University of London), for letting him consult his *Stalin and His Hangmen* (2004).
Grateful thanks are also due to John Montgomery of The Royal United Services Institute for Defence and
Security Studies, to the London Library, the Institute of Contemporary History and Wiener Library
and The Imperial War Museum. I am especially grateful for research and editorial assistance provided
by John Crossland and by my wife Joyce Rackham.

CONTENTS

CHAPTER 1

BLUEPRINT FOR TERROR

Arrests, tortures and executions in Russia originated long before the advent of Stalin. The Tsars, notably Ivan IV ('the Terrible') and Peter I ('the Great') secured their supremacy by rooting out all opposition.

The rule of Josef Stalin (1879–1953), and its grim legacy, will forever be central to the blood-stained saga of Russian political violence and terror. Following the death in January 1924 of Vladimir Ilyich Lenin, the architect of the Communist Party and of the Comintern (the Communist International, founded in March 1919), Stalin sought to extend his personal power by driving through a succession of Five Year Plans for enforced economic modernization. These were to bring about what amounted to a new Russian revolution, proving infinitely more brutal than the one which had brought down the Tsars.

Repression was engineered through show trials, tortures and executions. The most potent terror instruments used by Stalin were lethal state security agencies, notably the secret police known as the *Cheka* (*Vserossiiskaya Chrezvychainaya Komissiya po Borbe s Kontr Revolyutsiyei i Sabotazhem* – Extraordinary Commission for Combating Counter-revolution and Sabotage). Dating from the days of Lenin, the *Cheka* had unlimited powers to arrest, try, torture and execute. Its successor, one of many under different titles and acronyms, was the blandly titled OGPU (*Obyedinennoye Gosudarstvennoye Politicheskoye Upravleniye* – Joint State Political Administration), employed in the early 1930s to implement mass collectivization and consequent deportations of kulaks (wealthy peasants).

Opposite: A figure of absolute power, Ivan IV, known as 'Ivan the Terrible', headed an army that secured both the safety of his realm and his rule over it.

The film-maker Sergei
Eisenstein envisaged
Ivan the Terrible, made
between 1944 and 1946,
as a trilogy, but he died
before starting Part III.
The first part, depicting
Ivan's struggle to hold
power, was a resounding
success, featuring a
stirring score by Sergei
Prokofiev and winning a
Stalin prize. But Part II
met with the Kremlin's
disapproval and was
banned until 1958.

IVAN THE TERRIBLE

Post-revolution Russia was not, of course, alone in the creation of secret
police organizations. Previous repressive measures, instituted under a
succession of Tsars, were closely studied by Stalin, keen on developing his
own terror network. Particular respect was accorded to the legacy of Ivan IV
(1530–84), dubbed '*Groznyi*' (Dread or Terrible), a repellent mixture of
sadist and mystic, and the first to bear the title Tsar. For all his absorption of
Russian Orthodox tenets, he was every bit as cruel, ruthless and tyrannical as
his sobriquet suggested.

    Stalin set out to study Ivan's considerable achievements in completing the
construction of a ruthless, centrally administered and highly disciplined state,
while securing unquestioning loyalty among his closest followers and near
devotion from his subjects. Additionally, he was shrewd enough to recognize
that the abolition of the Tsars and the suppression of the Orthodox Church
had left a vacuum. Stalin, eventually to be characterized as 'Our beloved
leader', went on to fill this void.

Among the most notorious forerunners of the *Cheka* were Ivan's *Oprichniki,* the secret police developed over the course of seven years. Ivan inherited many of the characteristics of his father, Vasily III, Grand Prince of Moscow, who had his barren first wife, Salomonia Saburova, seized, beaten and incarcerated in a convent. Those who dared to side with her were summarily banished.

Murmurs of disapproval came with Vasily's subsequent marriage to Helena Glinskaya, the daughter of a Catholic Lithuanian refugee family. To the boyars (the traditional aristocracy), this was tantamount to insulting the Orthodox faith. The birth of Ivan on 24 August 1530 and his baptism at the Monastery of the Holy Trinity was, according to legend, marked by a roll of thunder that shook the heavens while lightning struck the Kremlin.

Three years later, on 24 December 1533, close on Vasily's death, the three-year-old Ivan was proclaimed Grand Prince of Moscow, Helena Glinskaya ruling in his name as Regent. The next few years were periods of violent intrigue among the boyars, many of them keen to sideline Ivan and seize the reins of government. The Regent faced the threat with measures that were to become all too familiar. Vasily's two brothers, Yuri and Andre, were seen as potential enemies and likely to appropriate the crown, in spite of their oath of loyalty to Ivan. Yuri was thrown into prison and died of starvation, while his brother was seized while trying to foment revolt, and reputedly poisoned. A bloodbath followed – mass hangings, lashings with the knout and the strangulation of those, including some royal princes, whose loyalty was in doubt. All of this did nothing to stem the discontent of the boyars, though the all too convenient death of Helena in April 1538 alleviated this somewhat.

> 'I adopted the devious ways of the people around me. I learned to be crafty like them.'
>
> —Attributed to Ivan IV

Ivan, just eight years old and already developing a quick intelligence, was at the mercy of the boyars, treated either with contempt or ignored altogether. He recalled some years later: 'Our boyars governed the country as they pleased, for no one opposed their power … I grew up … I adopted the devious ways of the people around me. I learned to be crafty like them'.

Moreover, from a young age he learnt to deal with opposition without mercy. On the occasion of a banquet at which he was expected to deliver a mere formal address, he went on the attack, accusing the boyars of taking advantage of his youth, pillaging his family's possessions and persecuting opponents. In particular, he blamed Prince Andrei, a member of the Shuisky family, who had seized one of Ivan's confidants, Fyodor Mishurin, skinning him alive and dragging him to the executioner's block.

A majority of the boyars, sensing a strong leader in the making, rallied to Ivan. Shuisky was seized, then flung into the street, where he was pursued and torn to pieces by hunting dogs. Ivan had tasted power and did not intend to relinquish it.

CRUEL EMPEROR

Instances of Ivan's cruelty and sadism increased, inflamed by bouts of heavy drinking. He was known to amuse himself by throwing cats and dogs from the Kremlin walls, tearing feathers off birds, piercing their eyes and slitting open their bodies. Treachery was seen everywhere. The most spectacular move towards securing still further power was a lavish coronation in which he was crowned 'Tsar and Grand Prince of All', a title derived from the Latin 'Caesar', translated by his contemporaries as 'emperor'. With his new office came a belief that he ruled by divine right. This was emphasized during the ceremony by Metropolitan Macarius, the senior bishop who was also his religious mentor and theology instructor. Invoking the strength of the Holy Spirit, he prayed: 'Grant him long days. Place upon him the seat of justice, strengthen his arm, and make all the barbarous people subject to him.'

The influence of the Metropolitan was considerable, encouraging the Tsar to make up for his earlier scant education at the whim of palace scribes. Urged on by Macarius, he devoured historical and spiritual texts with feverish impatience, seeing himself as a devout churchman, scrupulously observing the complex rituals of Russian Orthodox services. None of this, however, stood in the way of his urge to create what he intended to be a lasting dynasty. Within a month of his coronation, he married Anastasiya Romanovna, whose Prussian family had long settled in Russia, and who

Muscovite archers formed the main defence against the threat of mass cavalry. Additional protection was provided by Russian armourers, who were foremost in developing the protective visor.

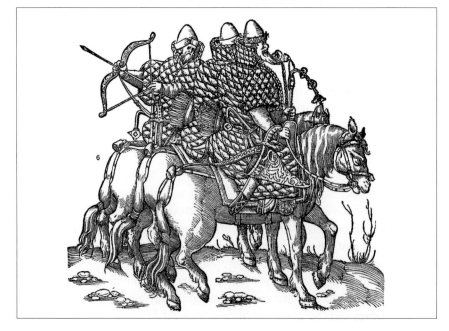

HARNESSING SERFDOM

Following his coronation in 1547, Ivan IV set out to remove a hitherto powerful hereditary aristocracy. A special police force undertook a terror campaign, resulting in the arrest and slaughter of hundreds. To replace the aristocratic system, estates were handed over as payment to landowners who were serving in the army or in government. Ivan, who could appropriate the rich estates at any time, was careful to ensure that they retained their value. Local peasants – known as serfs – had to remain on and farm the land.

This was possible by strengthening a legal code originally devised by Ivan III (1440–1506), to ensure the dependency of the peasants and restrict their mobility. Flight became a criminal offence.

Furthermore, serfs, possessing virtually no rights, were placed on the same level as goods and chattels. A landowner had the right to transfer a serf to a fellow landowner, while keeping the serf's personal property and family.

Except for the Baltic provinces, serfdom was not abolished until 1861 when revolt was already stirring, encouraging the view of Tsar Alexander II (1818–81) that it was better 'to liberate the peasants from above' rather than wait until they won their freedom by risings 'from below'.

Despite the emancipation, peasants who had originally run away from their masters could be arrested and punished for a decade beyond the year of abolition.

coincidentally was to become a great aunt of the first of the Romanov tsars. It was a marriage that lasted 13 years and was one of many – the exact number has never been established.

Ivan then lost no time in embarking on the sort of measures that have characterized tyrants down the generations. Essentially, these were either the removal or emasculation of the slightest vestige of opposition. Prominent in his sights were the detested boyars. A so-called 'Chosen Council' of selected favourites set in train moves to limit the powers of the hereditary aristocracy, in favour of a class of gentry who held their estates as compensation for service to the government and who owed their survival and privileges to the Tsar. This means of ensuring loyalty also had another motive: the estates had to be kept in good order. For this purpose, there was a convenient workforce to hand. These were the peasants who, already having their homes there, were obliged now to work for the new gentry and, of course, for the Tsar himself. It was a further consolidation of power.

EXPANSION

Another source of anxiety for Ivan were the Tartars, originally Asiatic Mongols, who made frequent forays into his territory. The threat was met by reorganization of the army, including the formation of six regiments of foot soldiers, or *Streltsy* ('shooters'). These were recruited for life, armed and equipped in European style and in some splendour. And the achievements of the Muscovite cavalry – men charging on wiry, unshod horses attacking with arrows, sabres and lances – were to become legendary.

When encamped in the meadows of the banks of the Volga near the strongly fortified city of Kazan, Ivan remarked on the 'unusual beauty of the walls of the fortress of the city'. Nevertheless, he proceeded to destroy them, along with mosques and palaces, in his 'holy war' against the Tartars. Most of the Tartars were killed, repressed or forcibly Christianized.

In 1552, Ivan and his forces set out for the town of Kazan; the fighting was marked by slaughter and butchery. Four years later, the Khanate of Astrakan, situated at the mouth of the Volga, was annexed without a fight. The coup was significant; the Volga from then on became a Russian river and the trade route to the Caspian was rendered safe.

This success was not enough for Ivan. Now that he had both banks of the Volga secured, he prepared a campaign designed to win access to the sea, something that had long been the aim of landlocked Russia. For all his obsession with grasping power in his own country, the Tsar was keen to establish trade with Europe, but this would be possible only with unrestricted access to the Baltic. Inevitably, he turned his attention westward and in 1558 went to war in a bid to establish Russian rule over Livonia (an area that includes present-day Latvia and Estonia). But Livonia's ally, Lithuania, proved a stumbling block, acting with Poland to gain the support of Sweden against Russia. For Ivan, the course of the Livonian war brought keen disappointment, and on a personal level too. Prince Andrey Kurbsky, one of his outstanding field commanders and a member of the Chosen Council, defected to Poland.

Ivan's reaction was predictable. Plainly, the humiliation over Livonia could be traced to either treachery or incompetence by the boyars and the field commanders. As became only too common, the methods of revenge exacted were a mixture of the cruel and the bizarre, designed in many instances to humiliate the object of the Tsar's wrath. The death of Tsaritsa Anastasiya, the mother of Ivan's six children, in August 1560 triggered the introduction of increasingly harsh measures since she had been able to exercise a moderating influence on her husband. This removed, Ivan accelerated his programme of repression, fuelled by fear that he could be the victim of a conspiracy to overthrow him.

Not for the first time, he decided on a particularly daring gamble. He announced that, in view of the extent of the boyar betrayal, he would abdicate as Tsar. With his new Tsaritsa, Maria, the daughter of Prince Temriak, a Circassian prince, he quit Moscow for an unspecified destination, later revealed as Alexandrovskaya Sloboda, some 47km (75 miles) north of the capital. There for a month he played a waiting game before finally sending off two letters. The first, directed to the boyars, consisted of accusations of crimes, betrayals and ill-treatment of the peasantry. No branch of the administration escaped. The army was to blame for the lack of defence from Tartar, Polish and German enemies. Not even the bishops escaped Ivan's wrath,

> Ivan accelerated his programme of repression, fearful he could be the victim of a conspiracy.

accused of siding with 'the guilty'. In the letter, he wrote, 'Therefore, with a heart filled with sorrow, no longer wishing to endure your perfidies, we have given up governing the country and have left to settle in whatever place God may lead us to.'

In fact, the missive was a shrewdly calculated political move; Ivan had no intention whatever of abdicating. The second letter, addressed to the citizens of Moscow, over the head of the boyars, made it clear that his anger was directed not to them but to the treacherous boyars. The letters were read to an assembled crowd; the results were electric. Widespread fury was directed against the boyars, now held responsible for the Tsar's decision to step down. There was also a deep-seated fear that, without a firm leader, the entire country could dissolve into anarchy. Faced with the threat of widespread civic violence, the current Metropolitan, Athanasius, assembled a delegation of princes, bishops, officers and merchants, and set out for Alexandrovskaya Sloboda to plead with the Tsar to return. They did not, however, receive a cordial welcome.

Fearful that they might include assassins, Ivan's guards closed in. Ivan, seizing the initiative, addressed the party by repeating his allegations against

During the reign of Ivan the Terrible, torture was the accepted and regularly used method of punishment. In fact, it became a spectator sport. To be torn to pieces by an animal was a penalty meted out to traitors, starkly shown in this painting by Vasily Surikov.

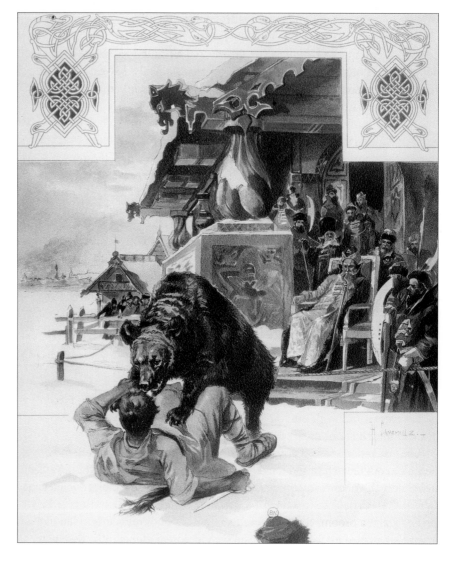

the boyars. Nevertheless, he declared, he was 'graciously' prepared to return to the throne.

Any relief that the suppliants might have felt was short-lived. He went on to set out his conditions: he demanded complete control over the punishment to be meted out to 'traitors' – a deliberately vague word that came to mean in practice the elimination of anyone who opposed his rule. Furthermore, dissidents would have their property confiscated, and punishment was to be extended to the families of 'traitors'. Once his demands had been made clear, Ivan prepared for his return to Moscow.

The Russian capital lay deep in snow, which in no way deterred the crowds. Gathering since dawn, they now fell to their knees in gratitude, weeping as their saviour passed. But if Ivan felt triumphant, he did not show it. The strain of the events that led to his return to power had clearly taken its toll. According to two Livonian noblemen, Johann Taube and Elert Kruse, who witnessed his return, Ivan was unrecognizable. Only 34 years old, he was wrinkled and grey, his brow furrowed: 'He had lost all the hair from his head and his beard'.

THE *OPRICHNIKI*

Despite the delirious reception he had received, he remained intensely anxious about the safety of his realm, his rule over it and even the institution of Tsardom itself. He reasoned that the only way to assure this was by the creation of a personal guard and of a heavily fortified headquarters within the Kremlin, from where he could operate.

This was designated the *Oprichnina,* a word derived from *oprich* (separate or apart). This was to amount to a virtual state within the state, ruled by Ivan alone, not as Tsar but as 'proprietor'. Its domain was vast: as well as the environs of the capital, it went on to swallow up 27 cities, 18 districts and all major routes of communication. The rest of the territory, the *Zemshchina,* was left to the boyars and former functionaries, but they were shorn of their previous powers and privileges.

Overall power was vested in the *Oprichniki,* the militia, the security force and secret police that soon became a byword for terror. Here was a highly efficient security machine, a blueprint for terror. Characteristically, these powers were never spelt out; they could be interpreted in any way their enforcer intended.

An increase in numbers came by stealth. A force of 1000 picked men swelled to 6000, each of them characterized by a propensity for ruthlessness and cruelty. Its operatives were black-uniformed men astride black horses, on saddles that carried the insignia of a dog's head, representing traitors to be removed, and a broom, for sweeping them out. A day's plundering, looting and raping was often followed by Ivan's invitation to dinner, followed by a mandatory visit to the torture chambers.

TORTURE AND EXECUTIONS

Executions by beheading were carried out in the Kremlin square next to the Church of the Intercession of the Virgin. Six boyars were among the first to fall to the axe, but a special fate was reserved for a seventh, Prince Dimitri Shevirev, who was impaled and reportedly took 24 hours to die.

Any criticism was interpreted by Ivan as an attack not simply on his honour but on the security of the state, an obsession which was soon to reach the level of paranoia. Under such circumstances, it is perhaps not surprising that historians have struggled to discover the first real example of protest. Most cite opposition in 1566 voiced from ranks within the

Zemshchina, who pleaded with the Tsar to abolish the *Oprichnina:*
'Our sovereign! Why do you order our innocent brothers to be killed? We all serve you faithfully and spill our blood for you. What kind of gratitude are you now showing us for our services? You have set your bodyguards on our necks, and they tear our brothers and kinsman from us. They insult us, beat us, stab us, strangle and kill us.'

The result was the arrest of some 300 noblemen, followed by public floggings, the wrenching out of tongues and a large number of executions. However, not all opposition could be disposed of quite so easily. In what turned out to be a serious miscalculation, Ivan appointed Fillip Kolychev, abbot of the Solovetskii Monastery, as Metropolitan, following the resignation of Metropolitan Afanassi, who had previously been the Tsar's confessor and who was a stern critic of the *Oprichnina.* Kolychev's appointment was not unconnected with the fact that two of his cousins served in it. However, if the Tsar felt that this ensured the other man's loyalty, he was soon disillusioned. Kolychev was prepared to use his position to speak out against an unceasing campaign of torture and murder carried out with not even the most peremptory of judicial processes. Moreover, he voiced condemnation during the course of his sermons, thundering on one occasion:

> Bribes and polite persuasion gave way to threats and arrests, followed by torture.

'In the most heathen and barbaric realms justice exists and there is compassion for the people. But in Russia there is neither. Our citizens go unprotected. Everywhere there is robbery and murder and these dastardly actions are carried out in the name of the Tsar.' When he went so far as demanding the abolition of the *Oprichniki,* the Tsar moved quickly to remove so potentially dangerous an opponent, whom he saw as representing a threat to the security of the throne itself.

HARD LABOUR

But Ivan had to recognize that this Metropolitan was too formidable a figure to be slaughtered in the manner of previous opponents. The *Oprichniki* were put to work. Their goal was to prepare the ground for the holding of a treason trial. The first step was the formation of a special commission, whose sole purpose was to amass as much compromising information as it could about Kolychev. In some ways, this proved easy enough: so contentious a figure did not lack critics and enemies only too willing to volunteer evidence which might help to ensure their own safety.

The commission next turned its attention to the monks of the Solovetskii Monastery, where Kolychev had served as abbot. Bribes and polite persuasion gave way first to threats and then to arrests followed by torture. As was expected, evidence was soon available on the former abbot's 'debauched life'. Paissy, the present abbot and an ambitious opportunist, was persuaded to testify against his predecessor. Kolychev calmly denied all charges but offered his resignation. Ivan, intent on stage-managing an infinitely more spectacular downfall for his opponent, refused, ordering Kolychev to continue with his religious duties until his fate was decided.

On St Michael's Day, 8 November 1568, in the Cathedral of the Assumption, the Metropolitan was officiating in his full sacerdotal robes when the service was interrupted. The *Oprichniki* burst in, disrupting the liturgy and reading the sentence of dismissal. Kolychev was stripped of his vestments along with his office and then flung in jail where, according to some accounts, he was later murdered.

The *Streltsy* paid a heavy price for rebelling against progressive innovations introduced by Peter the Great. These, it was felt, did nothing to halt serfdom, oppression and the hardships of military service. Their protests, though, brought only prolonged torture followed by execution.

THE *STRELTSY*

The *Streltsy*, from the Russian 'Strelyat' meaning to shoot, were possibly the world's first uniformed standing army, founded by Ivan the Terrible at the end of the sixteenth century.

A man served in one of four regiments, each of which had its own uniform colour and was provided with a wide variety of weaponry. Duties went beyond conventional soldiering: each man was also required to perform such duties as policing in cities and fire-fighting. The *Streltsy*, with their freedom from taxes, received money and bread allowance from the State Treasury. In certain areas, they were granted plots of land.

At the end of the sixteenth century, there were some 25,000 *Streltsy*, rising to 55,000 by 1681, including 22,500 in Moscow alone. They figured prominently in the siege of Kazan in 1552 and the Livonia war, but by the second half of the seventeenth century their efficiency compared unfavourably with that of the conventional regular soldier.

Their conditions of service deteriorated, leading to rebellions that were ruthlessly suppressed by Peter the Great. Gradually, *Streltsy* were incorporated into the regular army, and ceased to exist by 1720.

NOVGOROD

Ivan turned his attention to the next source of opposition, centred on the city and province of Novgorod, which lay in the north-west of the country on the Volkhov river below the outflow from Lake Ilmen. One of the oldest of the Russian cities, it had flourished not only as a sophisticated trading centre but as the key political and economic hub in the north-west. Consistent in its opposition to the rule of Moscow, dating from the fourteenth and fifteenth centuries, it had sought help from Lithuania. This had led Grand Duke Ivan III to seize some of its northern territories, forcing it in 1478 to recognize Moscow's sovereignty. Now, nearly a century later, the Tsar had wind of a plot against him, seemingly involving the entire establishment – aristocracy, church, court, and judiciary, with elements intent on surrendering Novgorod to the King of Poland.

Just how sound the Tsar's case for invasion really was has never been established. But the pretext was there, and he used it to leave Moscow accompanied by Ivan, his 15-year-old son, the *Oprichniki* and the army – including 1500 *Streltsy*, supported by cavalry and a corps of artillery. All towns between Moscow and Novgorod came under the lash, but it was the city itself that fared the worst in what was probably the cruellest reign of terror unleashed by the Tsar. A special court of interrogation turned out to be a pointless formality. The city was first surrounded by a high stockade erected by the troops. Abbots and monks were seized and beaten to death. Torture and executions stretched over weeks, with women and children being tied to sleighs, dragged through the streets and thrown into the icy and corpse-choked river. Revenge for treason, whether real or imaginary, was not the sole reason for the expedition into Novgorod. There was also a practical motive: the need to swell the coffers of the *Oprichnina* by plundering treasure and exacting fines from cathedrals and churches by way of tribute. Those who were not summarily executed were dragged back to Moscow for show trials.

Inevitably, news spread beyond Russia by way of crude, hastily concocted pamphlets, which were widely circulated. One was accompanied by an engraving of an obese and greying Ivan astride a throne flanked by mountains of corpses. There was a real danger that such reactions could jeopardize relations with other countries whose support was vital, notably Poland and Lithuania. Additionally, Ivan cannot have been blind to the signs that hatred and dread of the *Oprichniki* were mounting at home.

Following the subjugation of Novgorod came two devastating years for Russia of bad harvests, followed by plague, both of which threatened to cripple the country. To make matters worse, Crimean Tartars took advantage of ongoing internal dissent to storm Moscow in 1571, ransacking and torching everything except the Kremlin. Surviving accounts claim that only 30,000 of the city's 200,000 inhabitants survived.

A good deal of his life shrouded in mystery, Boris Gudunov was tsar from 1598 to 1605. However, he was the de facto ruler of Russia from 1584, as the regent for Ivan's younger son, Feodor I, who was married to Boris's sister. According to some accounts, Boris ordered the murder of Feodor's younger brother and heir, Dimitri, to secure the succession for himself.

CONCILIATORY GESTURES

There was a clear need for some gesture of conciliation with Ivan's increasingly restless subjects. In a bid to assuage possibly dangerous opponents, he abolished the term 'Oprichniki'. On the surface at least, he appeared generous; pardons were handed out to previous dissidents and some expelled noblemen were permitted to return to their hereditary lands.

Across Russia, widespread relief greeted the removal of the sinister horsemen with their dogs' heads and brooms. There was universal hope that a long-awaited peace and justice could be restored. But any changes were superficial. Ivan bided his time, hoping that his actions had quietened any likely opposition. The honeymoon did not last long. Within months of a proclaimed disbandment of the *Oprichniki,* a major political trial of prominent 'treasonous' boyars was mounted, followed by their execution. Jerome Horsey, an English statesman and envoy of Queen Elizabeth I, on a visit to Russia, witnessed a fresh round of tortures and executions, noting also that the Tsar continued to be surrounded by carefully selected favourites and henchmen. A new decree of 1582 specifically identified the most serious political crimes as those directed against the life of the sovereign himself.

Meanwhile, Ivan remained prone to megalomania, mistrust and bouts of sadism. His virtually uncontrollable rages – 'he foamed like a horse' according to one witness – had their most serious consequence when, on 19 November 1581, he became angered at the sight of his son Ivan's pregnant wife, Elena Sheremeteva, dressed in 'immodest' clothing. Accounts of the incident are contradictory. The most commonly told account suggests that, in the act of beating the woman, he was tackled by his son. Losing his temper, he struck him on the head with an iron-tipped staff and killed him.

> 'We, Peter the First, Emperor and Autocrat of All Russia … Peter the Great, Father of the Fatherland, Most Gracious Lord.'
>
> —Peter I

After that, the clock was ticking for Ivan, his health declining so rapidly that eventually he had to be carried on a litter. His decline was paralleled by that of Russia itself. By the time of his death in 1584 – occurring, it was said, while he was preparing for a game of chess – the prolonged and unsuccessful Livonian war had, along with incursions by the Tartars, overextended the country's resources, bringing it to the verge of economic collapse.

IVAN'S SUCCESSORS

The elaborate machinery of espionage, geared to rooting out traitorous elements, became the tool of Ivan's successors. His heir, the feeble-minded son Feodor, died childless, and the new tsar, Boris Gudunov, employed retinues of spies to monitor the continued activities of the boyars. Such suspicions were also shared by Mikhail Romanov (1596–1645), elected the first Tsar of the house of Romanov.

His successor and son Alexis (1629–76) set up a highly efficient Bureau of Secret Affairs, with agents penetrating into the very heart of the Duma (council of state), spying and reporting on its members and reporting military leaders and even foreign ambassadors. Keen to preserve all the trappings of autocratic rule, Alexis hand-picked a network of agents whose task was to shadow him on his travels and, more crucially, to penetrate the newly established foreign postal service. Letters from abroad were first delivered to the Foreign Office, where they were routinely slit open and all worthwhile information passed on.

PETER THE GREAT

With the death of Alexis and the eventual accession of Peter I ('the Great') (1672–1725), the Bureau, officially at least, ceased to exist. But predictably, it metamorphosed, this time under the starkly unambiguous title of the

Special Office of the Tsar, who termed himself: 'We Peter the First, Emperor and Autocrat of All Russia'. The preamble to edicts proclaimed: 'All-Illustrious, Most Sovereign, Emperor and Autocrat, Peter the Great, Father of the Fatherland, Most Gracious Lord'. With the advantage of dark glowering features, a towering height of 2m (6 ft 7in) and titanic energy, Peter became a master of intimidation. Power was exercised rigidly by the Special Office, which was under permanent orders to investigate the strength of individual loyalties and probe the activities of anyone suspected of treachery.

Peter's interests were by no means confined to his homeland: he was possessed by an insatiable curiosity about many aspects of Western culture. On several trips outside Russia, he travelled in disguise. It was a habit with one dangerous inherent weakness: it left the country ungoverned, often for months a time, a sure invitation to revolts and rebellion.

On more than one occasion, dissenters were the *Streltsy,* who had grown in power since Ivan's day, even to the extent of seeking to replace Peter by

Possessed of a towering temper, Peter the Great continued to mete out revenge for the rebellion of the *Streltsy* and for many other crimes. A contemporary diarist, Von Korb, wrote: 'No day, holy or profane, were the inquisitors idle; every day was deemed fit and lawful for torturing. There was as many scourges as there were accused and every inquisitor was a butcher … The whole month of October was spent in lacerating the backs of culprits with the knout and with flames … or else they were broken upon the wheel, or driven to the gibbet, or slain with the axe.'

Peter I of Russia – Peter the Great – was crowned Tsar of Russia in 1682 and Emperor in 1721. One of the country's most progressive rulers, he instigated a series of reforms that put Russia among the major European powers.
He opened up Russia to the West through two-way exchanges: key European engineers, shipbuilders, architects, craftsman and merchants came to Russia, while hundreds of Russians were sent for an education in Europe.
Peter was the first to organize a regular Russian army and navy.

his sister Sofia, regent at the time of his succession in childhood. Their fate included being burned to death amid piles of logs filled with straw or the lopping off of hands and feet preparatory to beheading.

An orgy of beatings, tortures and killings eventually put paid to the *Streltsy*, which had been the only truly effective opposition. In their place, Peter now had the chance to create elite guards regiments, consisting of men of unquestionable loyalty trained along Western lines. Another method of attracting loyalty was to facilitate some middle-class promotion to the ranks of the nobility; the purpose was to relegate the boyars to history.

With the change in the status of the nobility, together with severe punishment for anyone who dared to question his endeavours, Peter initiated a whole package of reforms that reached into every field of national life – administration, industry, commerce, technology and culture. By the time of his death in January 1725, he had created a blueprint for tyranny that, together with the example of Ivan IV, was to influence the early Communists. Indeed, following the abolition of the house of Romanov, Communist leaders singled out the two tyrants for praise.

STALIN'S ROLE MODEL

Stalin held up both Ivan the Terrible and Peter the Great as acceptable models of reform, although Peter was criticized by the Soviet tyrant for indecision when it came to annihilating the 'great feudal families'. By far Stalin's strongest praise, however, was reserved for Ivan, strikingly illustrated by his reactions to the two-part film biography, *Ivan the Terrible*. This was the work of the Russian director Sergei Eisenstein, who had earlier been celebrated for the film *Battleship Potemkin*. Part One of *Ivan* was acceptable to Stalin, but he condemned its sequel in terms that have survived in the records of the Central Committee of the Communist Party.

These convicts in Siberia, seen in 1892, would have been exiled under the Tsarist regime for committing offences serious or minor, criminal or civil. Because these penal colonies were so remote, escape was thought impossible. When the Communists came to power, most of the prisoners were exiled for committing political offences, such as treason, espionage, sabotage or anti-Soviet propaganda.

The demoralized director, suffering from what was to prove a fatal cardiac complaint, was summoned to appear before Stalin. He tried to defend himself against the accusation that he had failed to emphasize the justification for Ivan's terror against the aristocracy or to stress the necessity for being ruthless. His argument did not convince. The Party records, echoing Stalin's opinion, state that: 'Eisenstein betrayed ignorance of historical facts … depicting Ivan's progressive army, the *Oprichniki,* as a

THE *OKHRANA*

The *Okhrana* ('Security Section') was the secret police agency of nineteenth century Tsarist Russia, and pioneered methods that were adopted not just by its Soviet successors, the *Cheka,* OGPU, NKVD and KGB, but by Hitler's SS in Nazi Germany. One particular measure originating from the *Okhrana,* for example, was the work of the apartment block spy, the *Blockwarte* who provided intelligence to the local *Gestapo.* Systematic registration of politically suspect individuals was routine in Moscow by the turn of the twentieth century and was used St Petersburg between 1906 and 1908.

The *Okhrana* – its best known title within Russia – pioneered what later became standard practice: the demand that identity papers be carried at all times and that the registration of dwellings, together with personal details on their inhabitants, be made mandatory.

Ensuring the well-being of the Tsar and royal family was entrusted to the *Okhrana's* Special Section, which drew its recruits exclusively from the Russian army. In 1881, following the assassination of Alexander II and the growth of the radical Populist movement, teams of specialists were formed to combat terrorism, socialists and assorted organizations deemed hostile to the State.

From its St Petersburg base, the *Okhrana* ran a string of offices throughout Russia and then abroad. Prominent was the Foreign Bureau, which opened in 1883 in Paris, prompted by the shift of revolutionary activity from the Russian Empire to western and central Europe. Russian police officials admired France's internal security service, the widely respected *Sûreté General,* and were quick to gain access to its files, either through official consent or undercover.

Extended Network

Many of the key Russian revolutionaries known to be based in Paris had contacts in neighbouring countries, which prompted the *Okhrana* to spread its network beyond France and penetrate their cells. Additionally, former revolutionaries who had been arrested were given the chance either to 'double' or 'turn'. Persuasion was often simple; there was the ever-present threat of jail, exile to Siberia and, in extreme cases, the *Okhrana's* own execution squads. At its peak, the Paris Bureau had around 40 detectives on its payroll and some 30 agents elsewhere in Europe, paying particular attention to publishers of underground seditious literature, paper forgers and those suspected of operating bomb-manufacturing factories, as well as to smugglers of weapons and explosives.

However, the *Okhrana* by no means had things all its own way. The French Assembly had its share of socialist and radical deputies, many sympathetic to Russian revolutionaries. Protests mounted and were followed by a demand that the Paris office be closed down. In 1913 the Russians complied, but this was mere subterfuge. Operatives simply carried on with their work undercover, hiring former *Okhrana* employees, along with willing hands who had left the *Sûreté.*

gang of degenerates reminiscent of the American Ku Klux Klan. Ivan, a man of strong will and character, is shown as a spineless weakling, as a Hamlet type … Ivan, was great, wise. Ivan seems a hysteric in Eisenstein's version.'

On other occasions, Stalin lavished praise on Ivan, declaring his subjugation of the boyars as 'progressive'. By then, the Soviet tyrant had learned from the ruthless tactics of his predecessors and, indeed, profited greatly from them.

Limited Terror

Although many of the *Okhrana's* activities were said to inspire its Soviet descendants, there were important differences. While the *Okhrana* could order summary executions by hanging or firing squad, it could do so only when faced with peasant risings and the declaration of martial law by Moscow. The deportation of political prisoners to Siberia required judicial sanction.

During Alexander II's reign, some 4000 people were detained and interrogated for political crimes, but few were executed. From the mid-1860s to the mid-1890s, only 44 executions were carried out in Russia, all prompted by assassinations or attempts on the life of the royal family and government officials. In sharp contrast, following Lenin's launch of the Red Terror in September 1918, the *Cheka* executed hundreds.

By contrast, during Stalin's rule, the murderous NKVD acted as judge, jury and executioner; between 1935 and 1941, some 10 million people disappeared into the Gulag and three million were executed. Furthermore, treatment of dissidents under Stalin was far harsher than anything done by the *Okhrana*. The novelist Leo Tolstoy was the best known dissident of his day, with the police of Alexander III keeping him under surveillance and censoring his work, bur not imprisoning him or refusing to let him travel abroad. Consider, by contrast, the fate of Alexander Solzhenitsyn who, during Stalin's rule, disappeared into the harsh internal exile of the Gulag Archipelago.

The *Okhrana* had targeted liberals and revolutionaries alike, considering both groups to be threats to the Russian autocracy, but its greater strength was later seen to be its infiltration of agents. In July 1913, Vladimir Ilyich Lenin (1870–1924) discussed this success with colleagues, including Ramon Malinovsky, leader of the Bolshevik Deputies in the Duma. It was agreed that somewhere an *Okhrana* agent with close Bolshevik contacts was in place. There certainly was.

Malinovsky, a former soldier and St Petersburg factory worker, had joined the Bolsheviks as an active organizer in 1905 but went on to fall foul of the police and was arrested for high-profile political activities. To the *Okhrana*, he appeared to be likely material for an undercover agent. Tempted by 100 roubles a month, he began handing over reports on Bolshevik members, the whereabouts of meetings and storage locations for illegal literature. His eventual cover – Lenin's support of him as a candidate for the Russian parliament, the Duma – was ideal. But it was blown apart by the Bolshevik ascent to power. His role as a spy was clearly established, following the seizure of *Okhrana* files. On the first anniversary of the revolution, he was dragged to the Kremlin gardens and shot.

In the wake of Malinovsky's eclipse and that of others, the early Provisional Government convened a special commission to investigate the organization, operations and methods of the Tsarist police so that there should be no repetition.

CHAPTER 2

DOWNFALL OF A DYNASTY

The year 1917 proved a watershed in Russian history, bringing the abdication of Tsar Nicholas II and the downfall of the Romanov dynasty. Lenin ushered in a new Soviet government, proclaiming the dictatorship of the proletariat.

The *Cheka* secret police, set up in December 1917, embodied many of the practices of its Tsarist predecessor, the *Okhrana,* notably in tackling political crime with blanket rights to search, imprison and exile. It was to become, in essentials, a blueprint for all the secret services throughout the Soviet era.

When Stalin, as General Secretary of the Communist Party's Central Committee, was well on the way to securing absolute power in the years following the death of Lenin, he was able to build on close knowledge of many of the practices of the *Okhrana.* Indeed, suggestions surfaced that Stalin himself had once fed information to it and that, in return, a blind eye had been turned to some of his revolutionary activities. Stalin's detractors claimed that, although he was arrested several times, he was never charged with any major offence. Furthermore, his escapes from exile seemed comparatively effortless. It was never explained, for example, how he obtained papers to cross the Russian, Finnish and Polish borders, or where the necessary funds came from.

Suspicions surfaced anew in April 1956 when the American *Life* magazine published a photograph of what purported to be an original document sent in 1913 from the headquarters of the police in St Petersburg to a local office in Siberia. The letter recounted the activities of Josef Stalin

Opposite: Lenin, on May Day 1919, addresses a crowd in Moscow in the square previously used by the Tsars to proclaim their decrees. A memorial was unveiled to Stepan Razin, a Cossack chieftain who had raised Volga peasants in revolt and who had been beheaded in 1672.

Alexander Kerensky (right) had a major role in toppling the Russian monarchy and proclaiming the republic. He served as the second Prime Minister of the Russian Provisional Government of 1917 until power was seized by Lenin in the October revolution. Kerensky lived until 1970, dying in exile in New York.

as a police agent and informer during the years 1906 to 1912. It bore the signature of a Colonel Eremin (sometimes spelled 'Yeremin') and became known as the 'Eremin letter'. Although it has been claimed that the letter was a forgery, suspicions remain among historians that there may be additional evidence implicating Stalin and that this may well remain in the Kremlin archives. But any rumours circulating at the time were swept aside in the path of events that led to the overthrow of the Romanovs. Violent discontent seethed throughout Russian society, not least among the peasantry in key areas such as the Ukraine, the Volga and Georgia. Taxes had been levied mercilessly to meet the cost of projected industrialization. Poverty became commonplace. Nonetheless, in the face of all this, Tsar Nicholas II (1868–1918) remained deaf to any calls for change, continuing to exercise supreme power in the manner of his forebears.

LENIN'S OBSESSION

All of this acted as a spur to Vladimir Ilyich Ulyanov (1870–1924), otherwise known as Lenin, founder of the Communist Party and the Third International (Comintern). He was fuelled by hatred of the Romanovs, which had been festering since he was a teenager and had learned of the execution in St Petersburg of his brother Alexander, who had been implicated in a plot to kill Tsar Alexander III. The achievement of revolution became an obsession. As the brother of a state criminal, the young Lenin had been closely monitored by the *Okhrana.* As a law student at Kazan University and later at St Petersburg he had gained a first-class honours degree, although it was known that he was more preoccupied with the teachings of the social and political theorist Karl Marx – precepts destined to become the ideology of the Soviet Union and in time Communist parties worldwide.

Under the shadow of the *Okhrana* and in periods of enforced exile, Lenin set out to gather supporters for what was initially a small centralized grouping known as the Bolsheviks, formed with the aim of attracting the peasantry, by far the largest section of the population. It was a move to fertile ground and soon became a source of anxiety to the more sensitive sections of the nobility and even within the imperial family itself. The need for change was obvious and only the Tsar, increasingly under pressure to abdicate or face removal, seemed unaware of it.

Crippling food shortages and poverty set off violent demonstrations on the streets of Petrograd (the former St Petersburg) during the summer of 1917. A flashpoint was the main street of Nevsky Prospect, where government troops opened fire on the crowds. The government effectively lost control, with defecting soldiers joining the socialist revolutionaries.

The year 1917 proved a watershed. As the events of World War I went from bad to worse for Russia, agitators under the labels of Bolshevik, Menshevik and Socialist Revolutionary, ran riot. On 23 February, the women of Petrograd (as St Petersburg had been renamed) took to the streets with shrill demands for bread, while troops, firing into crowds at the behest of the Tsar and the *Okhrana,* mutinied when ordered to shoot to kill. Strikers and their organizers gained the upper hand. The cabinet resigned on 27 February 1917. Within days, Nicholas had abdicated, writing bitterly in his diary: 'All around me treason, cowardice and deceit.'

An assembled committee set up a Provisional Government, with Alexander Kerensky (1881–1970), a Socialist Revolutionary lawyer and accomplished orator, as First Minister. This was far from being good enough for the Bolsheviks, who had prepared their ground well. A number of their leaders managed to return from exile, but it was not until Lenin came to Petrograd that they became fully effective. His arrival there was made possible by the Germans, who allowed him free passage home from Switzerland, where he had been trapped in exile. They reasoned that he would serve to disrupt the country's war effort, making it vulnerable to defeat. Thus he was allowed to pass through Germany in a sealed train, arriving in Petrograd in April.

> 'All around me, treason, cowardice and defeat.'
>
> —Tsar Nicholas II, on being forced to abdicate

PROVISIONAL GOVERNMENT OVERTHROWN

Another milestone in Russia's progression to totalitarianism and its attendant oppressions was the overthrow on 25 October 1917 of the Provisional Government in Petrograd and the eclipse of Kerensky, no match for the ruthless Lenin. A Military Revolutionary Committee ensured a decisive takeover. A government headed by Lenin was swiftly established with a significant role for Leon Trotsky (1879–1940), a Jewish former journalist who had become Chairman of the Military Revolutionary Committee of the Petrograd Soviets and who assumed the title of President of the Soviet of the Commissars, presently shortened to *Predsovnarkom.*

Lenin's Bolsheviks held the real power, changing their name in the following year to the Communist Party of the Soviet Union. It eventually moved the seat of government and the Russian capital from Petrograd to Moscow. Lenin's committee had 13 members, the most junior of whom was made Commissar of Nationalities. This was Josef Vissarionovich Stalin (1879–1953), later to be promoted to a comparatively minor bureaucratic post at the Workers' and Peasants' Inspectorate.

Lenin's Bolsheviks set about releasing a stream of economic decrees and policies, all of which proved disastrous, resulting in devastating famine and plunging living standards. In the face of hyper-inflation, the population turned to bartering goods. Ration cards replaced roubles as the means of acquiring a family's essential supplies. Workers reasoned that if money could no longer buy goods, there was no point in working. Strikes became commonplace, and the government resorted to forced labour, adopting the methods it already used for drafting recruits into the Red Army. Workers and technical specialists already needed in sections of the economy were 'mobilized for military service'; those who refused to work or who left their jobs were treated as 'labour deserters', their punishments ranging from publication of their names to confinement in concentration camps.

CREATION OF THE *CHEKA*

The moves towards enforced recruitment of labour was blandly described by Bolshevik spin-doctoring as 'self-organization of the working class'. In fact, the merest whisper of opposition had Lenin punching hard in the face of unrest and threatened strikes, leading to the creation of what he called 'a special apparatus'. This, in December 1917, was the *Cheka,* headed by Felix Edmundovich Dzerzhinsky (1877–1926), member of a well-to-do family of Polish landowners turned ardent Marxist. It evolved as the strong arm of the Bolsheviks following the outbreak of the Russian Civil War in 1918. One of the causes of the conflict arose from the Bolsheviks' insistence on ruling alone, spurning cooperation with other socialist parties and shutting the door on free elections. Another source of unrest among dissidents was the Treaty of Brest-Litovsk, which had been signed by Lenin and Trotsky in the face of a rapid German advance, ceding much of the Ukraine and the Baltic states to Germany.

There was also the prospect of the advance towards the Urals of the so-called 'Whites', a loose confederation of counter-revolutionary forces made up of those who opposed the Bolsheviks. Their presence prompted the fear that they might attempt the release of the former imperial family, then being held in Yekaterinburg. On 17 July, the order went out to murder the Tsar, the Tsarina, their children and servants.

Leon Trotsky, once second only to Lenin and responsible for building up the Red Army, lost out to Stalin in the struggle for power. After the death of Lenin, he was thrown out of the party. By 1929, he was homeless and in failing health, seeking refuge in Europe but ending up in Mexico.

STALIN'S EARLY LIFE

Only adopting the surname of 'Stalin' (meaning 'steel') in 1912 when he was in his thirties, Josef Vissarionovich Djugashvili was the son of a drunken cobbler and a devout Christian washerwoman, born in the staunchly anti-Tsarist, provincial town of Gori in Georgia. The fact that his survival as a leader in later life was buttressed by intimidation, cruelty and terror may well be traced to the circumstances of his childhood. His father, Vissarion Ivanovich, whose ill-temper was frequently inflamed by drink, was said to beat both his wife Catherine and son violently. In later life, however, Stalin, possibly to give the impression of a stable background, strenuously denied that he had been ill-treated at all.

Accounts of his early life, possibly concocted later for propaganda purposes, need to be treated with caution. It was claimed, for instance, that when he appeared in a school play, Prince Galitzin, Tsarist viceroy of the Caucasus, told him that one day he would be a great singer. The boy replied indignantly that he did not wish to be a singer, wanting only to join the Georgian freedom fighters in the mountains. One of his heroes was Koba, a Robin Hood-type figure who attacked the landlords on behalf of the Georgian peasants. Here the testimony of a school friend, Josef Iremashvili, has survived: 'He wanted to become another Koba, a fighter and a hero as renowned as Koba himself.' What is indisputable is that the nickname Koba survived; use of it became strictly the preserve of his closest intimates in later life. At the age of seven, he contracted smallpox, but reserves of physical strength – later to become a byword – enabled him to survive while later enduring taunts of 'pock'. Catherine, deeply religious, took in washing and worked as a cleaner so as to keep her son at school and have him trained for the priesthood. A hard worker by all accounts, at age 15 he won a free scholarship to the Tiflis Theological Seminary where his devotion was not to Christianity but to the teaching of Karl Marx and other strictly forbidden texts. In 1899 he was expelled for revolutionary activity, rather than, as his devoted mother maintained, for reasons of ill health.

Depending on casual work and his friends for handouts, he drifted eventually to the Georgian branch of the Social Democratic Party, which sought the overthrow of the Tsar and the introduction of socialism. But all too soon, the *Okhrana* secret police had the party in its sights. Josef Vissarionovich, initially absent from his lodgings when the police came to arrest him, went into hiding and joined what became known as the 'underground resistance' to the Tsar. He spent his time writing articles for the socialist Georgian newspaper *Brdzola Khma* ('The Echo of Struggle'), as well as giving out leaflets and organizing strikes. Josef Vissarionovich was prepared to bide his time; it was apprenticeship for a lifetime of revolution.

RED TERROR

Originally, the powers afforded to Dzerzhinsky and his *Cheka* had been strictly circumscribed. Its immediate task had been to control the outbreak of banditry, looting and raiding of liquor stores that followed the seizure of power. But soon it was taking on the broader functions of a security police, dealing with all groups whose loyalty could be considered suspect. This took in bourgeois 'class enemies', officials of the former regime and Provisional Government and members of the opposition political parties. Through the so-called Red Terror, sanctioned by the People's Commissars, Dzerzhinsky's unconfined brutality made him the role model for all future Soviet secret police chiefs. Against him, the main opposition grouping, the Socialist

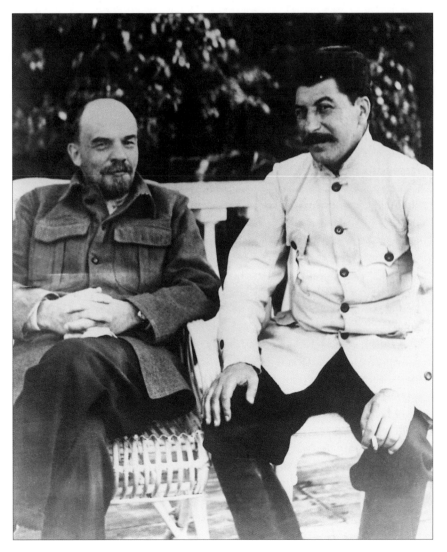

A rare moment of calm between two political antagonists. At the time of the attempt on Lenin's life, Stalin declared him to be 'the greatest revolutionary, tested leader and teacher of the proletariat', but on 24 January 1923, the year before his death, Lenin had written: '… I propose to the comrades to find some way of removing Stalin … and appointing somebody else who differs in all respects … Someone more tolerant, more loyal, more polite and considerate to his comrades.'

Revolutionaries, mounted a street demonstration in July 1918. The *Cheka* turned its guns on the group, killing 350 of its members.

Retaliation came to the streets notoriously on 17 August 1918, when Moses Uritsky, Jewish chairman of the Petrograd *Cheka* and one of Dzerzhinsky's most trusted acolytes, was gunned down outside his office, dying within an hour. Dzerzhinsky, assembling his *Cheka* cohorts, hurried to Petrograd, eventually tracking down the assassin, Leonid Kannegiser. A young Jewish poet, he justified the killing by declaring his hatred of the Bolsheviks, who as well as having killed a friend of his, had signed the traitorous Treaty of Brest-Litovsk. Furthermore, he declared that he had also intended to kill fellow Jews who had signed up with Lenin and that his shooting of Uritsky was intended to serve as a warning to them.

The killing panicked Lenin's followers. Among them was Yakov Sverdlov (1885–1919), also a Jew and a close ally of Lenin, who had played an important role in persuading leading Bolsheviks to accept the abolition of the Constituent Assembly, an elected coalition of various political groups. Now, Sverdlov, fearing the start of a general uprising and attendant blood-letting, urged Lenin to cancel further engagements. He was met with a firm refusal.

At first, Lenin opposed violent reprisals for the Uritsky killing, but he was soon to change his mind. Uncertainty continues to surround the identity of the person who fired at him on 30 August 1918, just as he returned to his car after speaking at the Mikhelson Factory in Moscow. Certainly, Fanny Kaplan, a former anarchist who had been sentenced to life imprisonment in Siberia for shooting a government official in 1907 and then released when the February Revolution overthrew the Tsarist government, was a prime suspect. On arrest, she confessed that she had intended to kill Lenin to show her support for the Constituent Assembly and disillusion with the Bolsheviks. Whether she acted alone or in concert with others was never established. The *Cheka* hoped to secure a statement from Kannegiser naming co-conspirators involved in the Lenin shooting. But, even after extensive interrogation, he revealed nothing and was shot. Kaplan too, was executed, her body said to have been thrust into an oil drum and burnt.

Whoever was responsible for the attack on Lenin had fired three shots. The first had torn harmlessly through his coat, the second had passed through his neck, barely missing the aorta, and the third had lodged in his left shoulder. Responsibility for the investigation rested with Sverdlov. A decree was issued reading: 'A few hours ago a villainous attempt was made on the life of Comrade Lenin. The working class will respond to attempts on the lives of its leaders by still further consolidating its forces and by a merciless mass terror against all the enemies of the revolution.' The mood was inflamed by *Pravda*, the Bolshevik newspaper, which parroted the party line at the behest of Sverdlov, fulminating, 'To the wall with all those who agitate against the Soviet power. Ten bullets for everyone who raises a hand against it'.

ORGY OF KILLING

There followed an orgy of killing under the direction of Dzerzhinsky's *Cheka,* which continued for around three years. The Petrograd *Cheka* was now under the direction of Uritsky's successor, Gleb Ivanov Bokii, a sexual pervert and sadist, notorious for arranging group sex sessions at his dacha (country villa) and forcing terrified female members of his staff to attend. Within a few weeks of the shooting of Lenin, he was reporting to Moscow with characteristic pride that 800 alleged revolutionaries had faced the firing squads and another 6229 had been imprisoned.

Bokii was but one of a number of sexual deviants and certified psychopaths who found their way into senior positions in the *Cheka*. Their recruitment was openly encouraged by Dzerzhinsky, who made sure they knew they were open to blackmail or indeed elimination if they stepped out of line. Another method of ensuring loyalty was simpler: 'class enemies' were denied access to ration books or to food shops unless they were prepared to serve the *Cheka*.

All killings received the enthusiastic backing of the injured Lenin, who urged the Bolsheviks to organize public executions 'to make the people tremble for miles around'. Furthermore, he favoured hangings rather than executions by firing squad, with corpses left to dangle in full view. Whenever a death sentence was decreed, the class enemy or counter-revolutionary forfeited his property to the *Cheka;* his dependants received nothing. In most

Opposite: The shooting of Moses Uritsky, a capable and ruthless organizer as well as a close friend of Lenin, came as a severe blow to the Bolsheviks. His death and eventually that of Lenin himself led to an orgy of violence which swept across Russia. Those slaughtered by the guns of the *Cheka* were deemed 'Capitalist hirelings', 'Criminal conspirators', Kulaks and White Guards. The campaign was orchestrated by *Pravda*, the party newspaper, which called for 'the death of the last capitalist, the last landowner, priest and army officer'.

In the wake of the shootings of Uritsky and Lenin, the *Cheka* turned vast tracts of Russia into killing grounds, notably in Petrograd, where armed bands were active on the morning of 8 November 1921, seemingly choosing their victims at random and making no attempt at concealment.

cases, execution meant a shot in the back in a cellar or garage, but not before the victims had been stripped naked and their clothes and valuables, including gold teeth, distributed to the executioners.

Understandably, accounts of the executions rarely survive. Vladimir Zazubrin, a deserter from the White Russians in 1918, recalled an incident whereby 'two men in greatcoats nimbly put nooses round the necks of the corpses, dragged them off to a dark niche in the cellar. Two others with spades dug at the earth … three men were shooting like robots, their eyes were empty, with a cadaverous glassy shine …' Torture was specifically legalized and the guidance issued: 'Physical pressure should be used obligatorily to known and obstinate enemies of the people as a method both justifiable and appropriate.'

On 5 November 1918, all sections of the *Cheka* were authorized to shoot 'class enemies' or isolate them in concentration camps. The basis for confining prisoners to these camps was a prime example of earlier policy being stood on its head. Originally, ordinary criminals had been released on the pretext that it was capitalism which had condemned them. All that was now swept aside. Now such prisoners were 'class enemies' who, along with others deemed as criminals, were confined in Northern Special Purpose Camps situated on the small Solovetskiye Islands on the White Sea and near Archangel on the mainland. Commitment to a camp followed a judicial hearing by the Judicial Collegium of the *Cheka*.

Although a criminal code existed to be cited in court, its paragraphs were deliberately vague, allowing them to be interpreted in any way the *Cheka* decreed. Defendants had neither the right to be present nor to defend themselves. Once an inmate of a camp, a prisoner became a commodity, owned by the government. On pitifully small rations and in the bleakest weather conditions, prisoners were used for highly demanding work such as digging canals. The number of camp inmates in 1920 was put at 50,000, rising to 70,000 a mere three years later.

The *Cheka* was also required to deal with the threat posed by advancing White armies, who were buttressed by support from invading Anglo-French forces. Methods for the disposal of surrendering White officers was carried out with a

> Death came by shooting, live incineration and drowning. Others were simply hacked to death.

brutality that clearly carried the mark of Bokii. With simulated friendliness and assurances of safe passage, the officers were handed free passes and summoned to 'register'. As they arrived to do so, the mood changed. Their fates were various: death came by shooting, live incineration (a method later favoured by the KGB against traitors) or drowning, the victims being thrown into the sea from barges. There were also instances of victims being hacked to death. The deaths of the Socialist Revolutionaries were particularly vicious, since Fanny Kaplan's sympathy had been with them. Other subjects of detestation were hauled out of their homes and promptly despatched.

LOYALTY TO STALIN

After the attempt on Lenin's life, those close to him knew what was best for them and were quick to profess their loyalty – among them, Stalin, who telegraphed to Sverdlov from Tsaritsyn (the future Stalingrad), exalting his leader as 'the greatest revolutionary, the tested leader and teacher of the proletariat'. In the meantime, despite his injuries, Lenin was able, in the short term at least, to fight his way to recovery. The problems he faced remained vast; opposition came, not just from the anti-Soviet Whites but from all the areas that the Tsars had formerly held, including the fertile Ukraine.

The end of the wars in 1921, however, did not satisfy Lenin; he perceived that it would offer a chance for opposition forces to become more dangerous. This was a view also held by the relentlessly ambitious Stalin, who for the moment at least maintained a low profile, presenting himself strictly as 'Lenin's mouthpiece'. However, with his appointment as head of the party's Central Committee, he had been handed the power base for his future dictatorship. His tentacles extended to membership of the powerful *Politburo*, which permitted him to expel 'unsatisfactory' members.

All the while, Lenin's grip had progressively slackened, as his health worsened. A succession of nervous headaches and fatigue progressed to partial paralysis and impaired speech. Even so, he observed with apprehension Stalin's growing overtures towards Trotsky. Calling on

FELIX DZERZHINSKY – 'IRON FELIX'

Today, a statue of Felix Edmundovich Dzerzhinsky once again stands in Moscow, appropriately in the courtyard of the headquarters of the police force at Petroka 38. Earlier, in August 1991, following the collapse of the coup against the then Soviet leader Mikhael Gorbachev by Communist hard-liners, the vast statue of Dzerzhinsky was forcibly detached by protesters from its plinth in front of the former KGB headquarters in Lubyanka Square and removed to an unspecified location. Like so many other Soviet monuments, it had been so sturdily constructed that a heavy-duty crane was required to complete the task. The preservation of the statue was seen by many observers to be sharply symbolic of the unwillingness by many Russians to eradicate the more potent memories of a violent past. This reluctance was confirmed in November 2005, when the request of a group of retired police officers for the bust to be returned was granted, despite widespread protests.

A Pole born near Minsk, Belarus, on 11 September 1877, Dzerzhinsky created the *Cheka* in December 1917, and had a career as a revolutionary which began when he was 20.

Leaving his education unfinished, he worked the factories and slums of Vilnius as a Marxist agitator, forming the Social Democracy Party of the Kingdom of Poland and Lithuania. His platform was to urge Polish social democrats to abandon Polish nationalism and parliamentarianism in favour of international revolutionary socialism. Arrested countless times by the Russian Imperial Police, he spent most of his early life in prisons, including a period in Moscow when he was clamped in irons, given a change of underwear once a fortnight, and forced to share a cell that was designed for 15 men with 100; tuberculosis was rife. These and other experiences in jail he later cited as an invaluable training ground. Instructions issued by him as head of the *Cheka* came to be based on the practices of his own interrogators and warders.

Louise Bryant, an American leftwing journalist who reported on the Russian Revolution, and who was a close observer of Dzerzhinsky, wrote that in appearance 'he is tall and noticeably delicate, with white slender hands, long straight nose, a pale countenance and the drooping eyelids of the over-bred and super refined. I never knew anyone who was a close friend … He asks nothing of life but to serve the cause of Socialism. Ease, wealth and happiness he puts behind him … He needs only to be convinced that his cause is righteous; nothing else matters'.

Save for Polish poetry and Marxist literature, his intellectual interests were said to be non-existent. Unlike Stalin and many of his closest colleagues, considerable reserves of strength, Lenin dictated to his secretary between December 1922 and January of the next year 'testaments' intended to support Trotsky and expressing doubt that Stalin was a fit person to exercise power. Within days of dictating the last of these testimonies, Lenin suffered a third stroke. Unable to speak or write, he lived on as a virtual corpse, dying in Gorki on 21 January 1924.

Dzerzhinsky lived a life of puritanical aestheticism, which in many respects resembled the conditions he had endured in his various prisons. He lived on mint tea and bread, wore a blanket for an overcoat and worked late into every night in an unheated office. Furthermore, his belief in the tenets of Bolshevism and Communism were doctrinaire and inflexible. On one occasion, he raged at his sister Altona for buying pancakes from a private trader and insisted that she threw them away. It was this sort of stance which earned him the nickname of 'Iron Felix'.

Dzerzhinsky once described the model Chekist as a man 'with a warm heart, a cool head and clean hands', a description that survived to be quoted in KGB training manuals. As Chairman of the *Cheka*, he was in absolute control. He was answerable at first to Lenin, with whom he shared an admiration for the French Revolution because both it and Bolshevism was 'a social system based on blood-letting'. As he grew into the office, he saw his task as hunting down and detaining 'the class enemy'.

Merciless Workaholic

A fellow Chekist had the task of founding *The Red Sword*, a journal that published statistics of executions, minutely tabulating such details as genders, social origins and dates of killings. A chronic workaholic who allowed himself little sleep, Dzerzhinsky spent his days compiling dossiers on those he considered to be possible 'traitors', even for the most trivial transgressions. Merciless

towards those who worked with him, his practice was to build up their workload with up to a hundred cases to process. When the agents, many of them fellow Poles, collapsed with exhaustion, they faced peremptory dismissal.

The end of the Civil War in 1922 led to the *Cheka* morphing into the OGPU, which was in turn absorbed by the NKVD. In contrast to the nomenclature, the security and intelligence apparatus of the Soviet Union remained largely unchanged. By 1924, Dzerzhinsky had become a firm supporter of Stalin, having been given control of the Supreme Economic Council and also elected as a candidate member of the *Politburo*. But worried colleagues were observing clear signs of a breakdown to his health, thanks to his heavy schedule: he insisted on travelling the length of the Soviet Union, minutely dissecting the efficiencies of the various branches of OGPU. Stalin was alerted and, concerned that his henchman was losing his effectiveness, ordered him to cut down his workload and seek medical attention. Dzerzhinsky paid little heed and on 20 July 1926, in the midst of a speech championing the peasantry during a Central Committee debate, suddenly collapsed. The cause of death was given as arteriosclerosis.

His status as a Soviet icon was preserved long after his passing, with giant portraits hanging in KGB offices and no less than six towns named after him as well as a museum dedicated to him at his birthplace in Belarus.

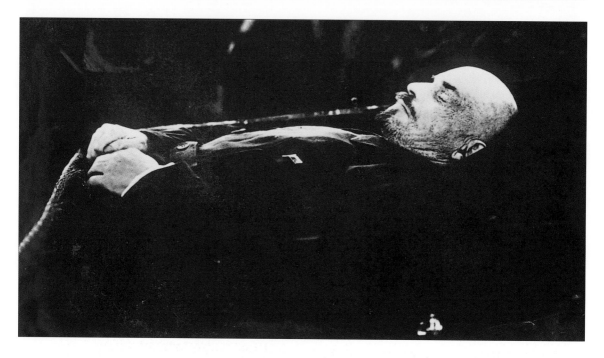

Lenin's body lay on public view in Moscow's Red Square. On the day of his funeral, sirens of thousands of factories, locomotive steam whistles and locomotive sirens were sounded all over Russia, while heavy guns pounded. Red Square was one vast sea of red flags. Black arm-bands edged with scarlet were worn by many, while the band played a succession of funeral marches.

ADVENT OF THE OGPU

Since the end of the Civil War three years earlier, the *Cheka* had become thoroughly loathed and feared, not least among Bolsheviks, a truth Lenin recognized. In order to achieve some semblance of revolutionary legality, the decision was taken in February 1922 to close down the *Cheka*. Its place was taken by a new security organization, the GPU (*Gosudarstvennoye Politicheskoye Upravleniye* – State Political Administration), which came nominally under the Ministry of the Interior. Capital punishment was temporally abolished and the functions of the GPU reduced officially to the investigation of civic crime, although its full functions as the state secret police remained, its members still being known as 'Chekists'. The following year came yet another title: OGPU (*Obyedinennoye Gosudarstvennoye Politicheskoye Upravleniye* – Joint State Political Administration). In order to curb violent excesses by freebooter elements who were hangovers from the days of the *Cheka*, central control, along with the formal creation of the Soviet Union, became rigid.

A Commissar of Justice was in overall charge, while political crimes had to be heard before Soviet courts and serious cases of treason before a military court. Traditional enemies from the old order – foreign spies and members of the old socialist parties – were pursued as before. Political power was now invested in Stalin who, having secured his own position, had gone on to outmanoeuvre any suspected rival, Trotsky included. Support was sought from two powerful left-wing Politburo members, Grigori Zinoviev

(1883–1936) and Lev Kamenev (1883–1936), who strongly suspected that Trotsky had his eye on the leadership and would dispose of them once he had secured it.

When Lenin had been unable to attend the Party Congress in 1923, Stalin took full advantage, moving swiftly to reinforce his hold and building up a body of supporters – a development which suggested that either he or Zinoviev could emerge as leader. One major problem Stalin faced after Lenin's death, however, was the very real possibility that his last statement would be published. Support for its suppression came from Zinoviev and Kamenev, who had also been criticized by Lenin. Stalin, however, was under no illusions about Trotsky, aware that he was dealing with no political hack but an organizer of proven ability and consummate ruthlessness. On joining the Bolsheviks in July 1917, Trotsky bestrode the Petrograd Soviet, seizing power during the October Revolution. Four years later, he had crushed the Kronstadt Rising when Petrograd sailors had called for the abolition of the *Cheka* and the Communist Party. Many had been shot for their heresy. Here was a formidable opponent; grounds for his removal had to be prepared with considerable care.

> 'Where force is necessary, there it must be applied boldly, decisively and completely. But one must know the limitations of force; one must know when to blend force with a manoeuvre…'
>
> —Leon Trotsky

An attack of malaria had sent Trotsky to the Caucasus for recuperation, an event that coincided with Lenin's death. Stalin then ensured that the funeral was held in Trotsky's absence, which left the ground clear for himself, Kamenev and Zinoviev to bear the coffin and deliver the obsequies. The pretence of sterling loyalty to the memory of Lenin was of course maintained until the end.

RIVALRY WITH TROTSKY

With a slow drip of rumour and insinuation, Stalin's next move subtly undermined his main adversary's achievements. Critical articles found their way to *Pravda,* claiming that Trotsky had once marked members of the Red Army for firing squads, including arbitrary shootings for those accused of retreating under fire. Opposition was also mounted to Trotsky's call for world revolution, with Stalin arguing instead that the priority must be to defend the communist system within the Soviet Union, a concept heralded as 'Socialism In One Country'.

It was not only Trotsky that Stalin had in his sights. Thanks to his growing power, he felt that he need no longer face the prospect of sharing power with Kamenev and Zinoviev. In contrast to Stalin, they also favoured the spread of Communism beyond Russia's borders. As supporters of Trotsky, they spoke out – and gave Stalin the advantage he was seeking.

The funeral of Felix Dzerzhinsky in Moscow on 20 July 1926. Seen second from the left is Alexei Rykov, first Commissar of the NKVD. Next to Rykov stands Leon Trotsky and Nikolai Bukharin is on Stalin's right. All three were later to be eliminated.

Both men were expelled from the Central Committee and muzzled into signing statements undertaking not to create conflict or give opposition speeches. Trotsky's refusal to sign brought inevitable punishment, banishment to the remote areas of Kazakstan.

In a bid to secure support, Stalin fastened on a longtime friend, Nikolai Ivanovitch Bukharin (1888–1938), who had become a member of the Bolshevik Central Committee within months of the October Revolution and had been termed by Lenin 'the darling of the party'. A flamboyant pragmatist who advocated the need for agricultural prosperity to provide a market for industrial goods, Bukharin called on peasants to 'enrich yourselves, accumulate, develop your economy'. Buttressed by Stalin, he was able, for a time, to establish a promising power base, even to the extent of replacing Zinoviev as Chairman of the Comintern.

But Stalin brooked no rivals. Bukharin, eventually realizing that Stalin was playing one faction off against the other and changing his theories to be rid of opponents, sought a meeting with Kamenev to suggest they should join forces to end the one-man dominance of the party. But it was too late; Stalin, the blacksmith's son, with most of his loyalist supporters in place and with an effective secret police machinery, had become the dictator of the largest country in the world.

SIDNEY REILLY

A group of *Cheka* agents, operating under the codename of 'The Trust', was behind one of the most celebrated espionage coups of the early Soviet Union. They posed as members of an underground Monarchist Association of Central Russia (MOR), intent on murdering Lenin and his associates. But the real aim was to trap the British agent Georgi Rosenblum, known as Sidney Reilly (1874–1925).

The brain behind the deception was Aleksandr Yakushev, of the OGPU, which had succeeded the *Cheka* in 1923. Using his genuine Soviet foreign trade position to pose as an MOR representative, Yakushev courted Tsarist and White Russian exiles. He eventually came across Reilly.

On the outbreak of World War I, Reilly had been sent to Russia. Later, in 1918 he had been accused of involvement in the attempted assassination of Lenin. He was found guilty of espionage and sabotage and sentenced to be shot. Narrowly escaping arrest by fleeing the country, his next intelligence involvement was in October 1924, resulting in one of the century's most notorious political forgeries.

Early that month, the British Foreign Office received a copy of a letter, purporting to come from Grigori Zinoviev, President of the Comintern, and addressed to the Communist Party of Great Britain. It urged the party to stir up the British proletariat with acts of sedition to inflame class war. Two major figures in British intelligence, Vernon Kell, the head of MIA (home intelligence), and Sir Basil Thomson, who led Special Branch, were convinced the letter was genuine but agreed to keep it secret.

In vain, as it turned out. The contents were leaked to two British national newspapers four days before the 1924 General Election. It was a major embarrassment for Ramsey Macdonald, the leader of the Labour Party, which was held to be pro-Soviet and in favour of an export loan to Russia to stimulate trade. The Conservative Party won the general election four days later; and established treaties between between Britain and the Soviet Union were summarily abandoned. Sir Stewart Menzies, future head of MI6 (Foreign Intelligence), later admitted leaking the Zinoviev letter to the press, while speculation grew that it had been concocted and forged by Sidney Reilly and Arthur Maundy Gregory, another MI5 spy.

On 26 September 1925, Reilly was deceived into crossing the Finnish frontier for a meeting with supposed MOR conspirators. He was arrested and incarcerated in the Lubyanka. Attempts to break him met with little success – at first. But his file contains a letter to Felix Dzerzhinsky, offering to betray British and American intelligence officers and to pinpoint Russian émigrés in the West. On 5 October 1925, he was driven to some woods for exercise. The car was halted, on the pretext of a breakdown, and Reilly was allowed to get out and stretch his legs. He walked some 40 paces before before being shot from behind. According to one report, he 'let out a deep breath and fell without a cry'. This is at odds with other accounts which claim that he fell to the ground still alive, was rolled over and shot through the chest. The body was conveyed to the sickbay of the Lubyanka prison, where agents filed past in triumph.

The Reilly file, released by M15, contains many documents, which confirm the accounts of his death. The file includes a six-page typed statement by an unidentified informant, thought to be a pro-Western Russian spy, who claimed: 'The Bolsheviks at first wished to conceal his arrest but the English somehow or other found it out and the Bolsheviks, in order to escape possible demands by the English for his release murdered him when he was taken out for exercise'. Legends about his prowess as a spy are prolific. However, there is by no means universal agreement about his effectiveness. A 1919 file from the US Bureau of Investigation (later the FBI) concluded by declaring he was a 'world class confidence man'. But to those entranced by the history of espionage in the 20th century, he remains 'Reilly, Ace of Spies'.

ПЯТИЛЕТКУ–В ЧЕТЫРЕ ГОДА!

"ЛЮДИ, БОЛТАЮЩИЕ О СНИЖЕНИИ ТЕМПА ЯВЛЯЮТСЯ АГЕНТАМИ НАШИХ КЛАССОВЫХ ВРАГОВ, ЯВЛЯЮТСЯ ВРАГАМИ СОЦИАЛИЗМА" (СТАЛИН) XVI ПАРТСЪЕЗД

CHAPTER 3

ROAD TO TOTAL POWER

Stalin, buttressed by agents of terror, stood as undisputed master of the Soviet Union. A series of ruthlessly enforced Five Year plans drove scores of Soviet citizens from their lands and into dire poverty.

Stalin, with total power in his hands, was quick to make sure that the OGPU continued evolving as the ultimate instrument of repression. From the start, Vyacheslav Menzhinsky, the soft-voiced and bespectacled successor to Dzerzhinsky on the latter's death, cultivated his own style, deliberately assuming a low profile, ruling as a bureaucrat from the shadows.

He was left in no doubt as to what was expected of him. In a speech to the party Central Committee in November 1928, Stalin first hailed the success of the new Soviet political system, which had outstripped the achievements of the advanced capitalist countries, and then outlined his next moves. He made no attempt to gloss over the truth of the Soviet Union's grim economy, declaring: 'In order to secure the final victory of socialism in our country, we must also overtake and outstrip these countries technically and economically. Either we do this or we will be forced to the wall'.

COLLECTIVIZATION

He reiterated an earlier concept of 'Socialism in One Country', by which he meant building permanently entrenched socialism without help from other nations. Russia at that time needed reliable grain supplies at low prices, in order to feed the increasing numbers of workers the state required. The only

Opposite: This poster was intended to ensure a prompt response to the problems of Soviet Russia's ailing economy and an implied warning to those who failed to deliver it. The poster reads: 'Five Year Plan in Four Years – People who blather about slowing down the speed are class enemies' agents. They are the enemies of Socialism.' It is signed by Stalin.

The forcible conversion – in reality, liquidation – of Kulak farms into state collectives meant entire families being expelled from their homes. A carefully posed picture of displaced Kulaks suggests that all departures were orderly affairs. In fact, those who resisted faced years in the camps. It is believed that around 10 million were deported.

way to make this possible was by the compulsory transformation of individually owned peasant farms into large rigidly controlled collectives. It was intended that this should be achieved through force.

The stumbling block to collectivization was the minority of the wealthier peasants, the kulaks – the 'tight-fisted' – who, hailing from late Tsarist times, were able to hold the state to ransom. In a free market, they could refuse to sell their grain if the price was too low and if there were no consumer goods to be bought. The OGPU was directed to prepare the path to collectivization by inflaming hatred for the kulaks; Menzhinsky set about recruiting the necessary personnel. He proceeded to seek out talent, not just from one-time members of the *Cheka*, but among the ranks of the bourgeoisie and intelligentsia whom Stalin had previously denounced. Even supporters of the discredited Trotsky were wooed. Under the *Cheka* and in the earliest days of the OGPU persuasion had been by fear and the bullet. Menzhinsky's approach, on the other hand, was through the promise of salaries and attractive inducements. Needless to say, such inducements were presented in such a way as to make clear that refusal would be decidedly unwise.

The remodelled OGPU was an essential component in the operation of a series of Five Year Plans launched by Stalin, in order that the state could acquire reliable deliveries of desperately needed grain. The kulaks' stance fuelled a general deep-seated resentment of the peasantry, who formed 80 per cent of the population and with whom the Bolsheviks had never come to terms. Menzhinsky despatched hand-picked agents into the villages to talent-spot peasants whose hatred of the kulaks was so bitter that they would be prepared, given the proper backing, to work against them. It was a move which received the full support of Stalin, who spelt out his intentions: 'In order to oust the kulaks as a class, the resistance of the class must be smashed in open battle.'

A decree entitled 'On the Means for the Liquidation of Kulak Farms in Areas of Complete Collectivization' swiftly followed. This listed the penalties awaiting those who 'actively opposed the socialist order'. The 'liquidation' of the kulak farms meant that these and their strips of land would no longer exist but would be converted into large collectives, if necessary swallowing up entire villages. In human terms, collectivization was to affect the lives of 20 million people living in 600,000 villages.

Twenty-five million peasant holdings were absorbed into 240,000 collective farms. The justification was that these farms would prove more efficient than small private ones. They would be provided with tractors and combine harvesters, equipment which, under the existing system, was beyond the means of the poorest peasants. Surplus labour would be switched to the needs of vital industries in factories, mines and construction sites. Private commercial firms would be swept away. Credit banks, peasant farms, retail shops and most of the artisan workshops were to be taken over. Quotas of grain and other crops were to be requisitioned, by force where necessary and at prices fixed by the state. All essential possessions – carts, farm implements, horses and livestock – would become state property. In some cases, individuals might be allowed to own a dwelling place and a strip of land, but this was a privilege granted on the whim of the local Soviet.

THE KULAKS

On 30 January 1930, Stalin struck. Another decree, 'On Measures for the Elimination of Kulak Households in Districts of Comprehensive Collectivization', was approved by the *Politburo*.

This seemingly happy, healthy collective farm worker serves as a convenient representative of Soviet propaganda. The truth was very different. Thousands of peasants endured a miserable existence, starving as their entire grain stocks were seized and the farms on which they worked converted into collectives.

VYACHESLAV MENZHINSKY

At first sight, the Pole Vyacheslav Menzhinsky (1874–1933) seemed an unlikely choice as the successor to Felix Dzerzhinsky as head of the OGPU. Indeed, he struck many of his contemporaries as a bizarre choice for any key Soviet position. It was something of a surprise that following the Revolution he had not been eliminated as a member of the ruling class, especially as his elder brother Alexsandr had been an auditor for the Tsar's Ministry of Finance. Indeed, in career terms, Menzhinsky could have been written off as a failure, a mere rolling stone who in the early 1900s had practiced law and dabbled in poetry, music and painting in between being a Bolshevik sympathizer. His family had connections both with Lenin and Stalin, but what he appeared to lack was the necessary commitment to revolutionary politics.

Indeed, in 1908 he came perilously close to digging his own grave, attacking Lenin in print for heading a political group he

Vyacheslav Menzhinsky in 1925: a one-time critic who became a survivor due to a knack of removing opponents while ensuring his own survival.

Kulaks were to be shot or imprisoned, with their families facing deportation or expulsion from their farms. A second category of kulak, considered the 'most dangerous and reactionary', was destined for detention camps located in what was described with deliberate vagueness as being 'distant areas'.

Just who were designated kulaks was up to the OGPU, which even went as far as penalizing villages too poor to contain any. An entire family in one Belorussian village was considered rich because it owned a cow and a mare with a foal. A female relative who had helped with harvesting was designated a servant in the pay of kulaks. A peasant owning eight acres was forced to clear the snow from railroad tracks, then deported, and his property seized.

described as being no better than a noisy gypsy camp, and suggesting that Lenin was twisting Marxism according to his own whim. At the same time, Menzhinsky was a choice opportunist of consummate ruthlessness, who swam with the tide, echoing the views of those likely to be of use to him, most notably in dismissing the peasant commune 'as one of the major breaks on Russia's agricultural development'.

Such tactics eventually came to the attention of Stalin, who was forever keen to foster rebels, not least because earlier indiscretions could at any time be used to topple them. Trading on his brother's banking experience and influence within the Petrograd Bolsheviks, Menzhinsky secured the job of Commissar for Finance. But far more to his taste was an intelligence-gathering post in the Ukraine, where nationalism thrived and there was always the threat of danger for the new regime. It was here that he gained the favour of Dzerzhinsky and a place in the *Cheka*.

In contrast to the dull uniform garb that had become mandatory for all Stalin's cohorts, Menzhinsky often cultivated the appearance of a bourgeois banker in a three-piece suit, right down to the bowler hat. A fastidious man, he took the keenest interest in methods of torture, execution and the way the condemned faced their last moments, but never attended an execution.

His health was poor, so he was incapable of standing or sitting for long. Cosseted by his deputy, Genrikh Yagoda, he conducted business from a divan, his legs covered with a rug. This gave him a useful edge at his interrogations, particularly as those he was questioning were thrown off balance by his appearance and posture. The air of menace was increased still further by his exquisite courtesy and an air of friendliness, which was especially marked when sending victims to their deaths.

As well as his activities during the period of collectivization, Menzhinsky was steadily building up his own power base, required by Stalin to stage show trials of those who had fallen from favour, particularly if they were considered to be on the Right. These followed the longterm character assassination of intended victims, including Trotsky and Bukharin. The former was driven into exile and assassination in Mexico, while Bukharin fell ultimately to a bullet in the back of the head.

By the summer of 1933, Menzhinsky's health had gone seriously into decline and, aged fifty-nine, he died in hospital of what was said to be heart and kidney disease. Later, it was declared that he had been poisoned with mercury vapour. Accused four years later of Menzhinsky's murder was his devoted acolyte, Genrikh Yagoda, who had been promoted to his chief's job and ultimately headed the newly formed NKVD.

Menzhinsky, at the behest of Stalin, saw his task as switching senior staff from their normal counter-espionage duties to concentrating on the activities of counter-revolutionary kulaks. His undercover work among his supportive peasants was paying off. One of them later revealed how kulaks were selected: 'Just between the three of us, the poor peasants of the village got together in a meeting and decided: "So and so had six horses …". They notify the OGPU and there you are. So-and-so gets five years.'

As the first phase of the Five Year Plan accelerated, the countryside faced steadily more draconian demands. Farmers in the region of Smolensk, located some 400km (249 miles) southwest of Moscow on the Dnieper river, were among those who took the full brunt. They lagged seriously behind in meeting the required quotas for producing grain. Total powers were given to appointed emissaries, who were required to extract grain from any sources and speed up delivery.

Not all the peasants resented the kulaks. There were those who respected them as village leaders, many of whom were relatives. Additionally, there was deep-seated resentment, some of it even from the local Soviet and party apparatus, at high-handed intentions to categorize all peasants as poor, middle or well-to-do. There were instances of deliberate obstruction; Menzhinsky's emissaries were denounced at village meetings as 'thieves and bandits'. However, repercussions were harsh. Grain quotas were stepped up sharply, with demands that deliveries be made in periods as short as two to five days. Jail sentences and forced labour were imposed for late or unfulfilled deliveries. Stocks were seized in raids on the homes of offenders, some of whom simply hid theirs or, in the case of the wealthier peasants, tried to bribe the emissaries. Villagers who sided with the opponents of the kulaks were dubbed 'sub kulaks' and set upon, their homes torched.

> 'The stations were lined with begging peasants … the women holding up to the carriage windows horrible infants with enormous wobbling heads, sticklike limbs and swollen, pointed bellies.'
>
> —Arthur Koestler, on the Ukrainian famine

Local militia forces were mobilized under the control of the local OGPU chief and sent to the current trouble spots. Prominent among these was the Ukraine; with its large population and fierce sense of nationhood, it was feared by Stalin, who recognized it as a threat to Moscow's rule. Around 10 million Ukrainian peasants were forced into collective farms. Orders were given for the area's entire grain stock to be confiscated. Borders were sealed, all movement forbidden and no food allowed to enter. Entire stocks of seed, grain, silage, and livestock were seized from farms. The once great breadbasket of Europe was steadily reduced to a desert.

FAMINE

Deaths from starvation were immeasurable. Those left alive turned to begging, and gnawing grass and tree-bark. When all sources of food were exhausted, cattle and horses were slaughtered. Only chickens and pigs remained. Of these, Vasily Grossman, a Soviet historian and journalist who later became disillusioned with the regime, wrote: 'The animals had become afraid of people and their eyes were wild. People boiled them, but were left with tough veins and muscles. And from their heads they made a meat jelly.'

Mass starvation started with the melting snow. Red Army troops and OGPU agents sealed roads and rail links. Deaths from hunger, cold and

sickness multiplied. For sustenance, people turned in desperation to rats, ants and earthworms. Soup was made from dandelions and nettles. For as long as they could, people huddled in their villages, but when there was nothing there for them, were forced out to squat along the rail tracks, begging for crusts to be thrown from carriage windows. Carts making for the streets of Kiev every morning picked up the corpses of those who had died in the night. The children were described by one witness as having 'thin, elongated faces like dead birds'.

Military units under OGPU command threw up rings of steel around the villages. Crude watchtowers were erected above fields, from where guards armed with shotguns picked off those who were driven by hunger to cut off ears of corn. A court in Kharkov handed out 1500 death sentences in a single month; a woman received 10 years' detention for cutting 100 ears of corn from her own plot, a mere two weeks after her husband had died of starvation. Where crowds gathered to protest, tanks and machine-guns opened fire. Those who escaped the massacres were herded into cattle trucks and deported to the slave labour camps of Siberia or the Arctic. Frequently, they were destined to spend weeks in these windowless trucks, which were so tightly packed that many prisoners did not feel the floor beneath their feet for

In the early 1930s, Ukrainian families endured malnutrition and total starvation. Villages were surrounded and laid waste, being put to the torch, attacked by tanks and artillery, and bombed from the air.

days. As for food, they existed on scant water supplies and a dubious diet of thirst-provoking herrings, dried carp or anchovies.

The future Nobel prize-winning writer Alexander Solzhenitsyn (born 1918), who was arrested for criticizing Stalin and sent to a labour camp in Kazakhstan, wrote of being entangled among bodies in one of the trucks and 'falling asleep to the clacking of the wheels without knowing whether we will see forest or steppe tomorrow. Sometimes we could judge from a snatch of sun whether we were being taken east or north'. As to the deportees themselves, it was not just the head of the family who was seized. 'They burnt out whole families and watched to be sure that none of the children – fourteen, ten, even six years old – got away … All had to go down the same road, to the same common destruction'. It was later estimated that between a quarter and a third of the deportees died, including the children.

GULAG

Responsible for the implementation of deportations was the largest division of the OGPU, known from its acronym as the Gulag (*Glavnoye Upravleniye Lagerei* – the Chief Administration of Corrective Labour Camps). This formed a vast network of penal institutions populated by slaves, making up as much as 10 per cent of the entire Soviet workforce. Hatred of the kulaks and the peasants was not the only motive for the camps. A workforce from them could be supplied to local mines and forests and worked to death at around a third of an average worker's wages.

Stalin sent in three of his most able commissars, Vyacheslav Molotov (1890–1986), Lazar Kaganovitch (1903–91) and Genrikh Yagoda (1891–1938), to destroy the remnants of opposition. Kaganovitch achieved the most conspicuous success, boasting weekly killings of some 10,000 Ukrainians. Those despatched to Siberia were at the mercy of one of OGPU's most vicious chiefs, Leonid Zakovsky, who prided himself on being the author of a widely used handbook on torture, giving details of what he considered to be the best methods. Zakovsky in his turn answered to Yagoda, who had joined the Bolsheviks in 1907 and had become a member of the presidium of the *Cheka,* taking charge of the Soviet Union's forced labour camps in 1930. Not the least of Yagoda's duties was ensuring that OGPU, and not the courts, dealt with those who dared to speak out against the methods used in collectivization.

The precise number of Ukrainians murdered by firing squads or dying through famine remains unknown. Records, later stored in KGB archives, point to at least seven million deaths, but some Ukrainian historians have put the figure in excess of nine million. A quarter of the Ukraine's population was exterminated. Six million other farmers across the USSR starved to death or were shot during collectivization. Those sent to labour camps on the White Sea canal or at the gold mines at Magadan, far to the north, perished

in the excruciating cold – a fate shared, incidentally, by their guards and the dogs. In addition, a fierce campaign was launched against the Orthodox Church, which stood at the very heart of peasant culture, forming a cornerstone in the community. Churches in the villages were closed and sacked, crosses and bells removed and destroyed, and countless numbers of monks and nuns deported.

Events in the Ukraine could not be concealed totally from the outside world, despite rigid internal press censorship. Western journalists, initially sympathetic to the cause of the Russian Revolution, were able to make tours of the collective farms and the surrounding countryside only under close official supervision. But soon reports were being fed to reporters by foreign engineers and technicians returning from the Ukraine. By no means all journalists accepted massaged news. The writer Arthur Koestler, visiting the Ukraine at the time, described seeing from his train starving children who 'looked like embryos out of alcohol bottles … the stations were lined with begging peasants with swollen hands and feet, the women holding up to the carriage windows horrible infants with enormous wobbling heads, sticklike limbs and swollen, pointed bellies.'

When the British journalist Malcolm Muggeridge, at first a Communist sympathizer, heard of the famine, he eluded the security net and travelled to

One branch of the NKVD was concerned solely with political prisoners, many of whom were incarcerated within the Gulags. These convicts, held in Siberia in 1931, are engaged on one of a number of building projects under Stalin's First Five Year Plan (1928–32).

VYACHESLAV MOLOTOV

Born in Kuarka, Russia, to middle-class parents, the Vyacheslav Mikhailovich Scriabin (1890–1986) joined the Bolshevik Party at the age of 16, later adopting many pseudonyms to dodge Tsarist pursuers, before settling for Molotov (from molot, ' the hammer').

After the 1917 Revolution, he rose within the *Politburo,* where he became a dedicated follower of Stalin, adapting himself to his leader's every need, not least his daunting working hours, which frequently stretched until 3 a.m. Molotov went on to become Stalin's chief of staff, a role that made him a combination of counsellor, technical adviser on foreign affairs and official spokesman for the Soviet Union worldwide.

As the cold hard-man of Soviet politics, Molotov considered ideology to be infinitely more important than human relationships, even if this compromised his devoted Jewish wife, Polina. Fiercely anti-Semitic, Stalin detested her and ordered her arrest in January 1949, along with members of her family and a number of associates. A sister and a brother subsequently died in prison. Molotov had no idea if she still lived and Stalin, who was assured of his loyalty, had no intention of telling him.

Outwardly Molotov remained imperturbable, continuing to serve his master, his vindictive streak intact. When death sentences were meted out to those denounced as traitors, Molotov was notorious for addenda written by hand below his signature, typical of which was 'Give the dog a dog's death!'.

No record exists of him seeking to moderate the purges or even plead for the life of individuals. Those who worked with him found him harsh and ill-tempered, later recalling that he showed no signs of pity for Stalin's prisoners. Bureaucratic exactitude was the first consideration. The American journalist John Gunther wrote in 1938: 'Molotov … looks and acts like a French professor of medicine – orderly, precise, pedantic. He is a man of first rate intelligence and influence. Stalin gives him much of the dirty work to do.' This assessment, however, seemed an overestimate to the Polish historian Isaac Deutscher, who described Molotov as 'slow-witted, dull but with enormous patience and capacity for work'.

Prior to their execution, condemned individuals had their personal details recorded on filing cards, with photographs taken on their arrest being added to the burgeoning NKVD archives. Forms recording each execution carried one simple instruction: 'When carrying out the sentence it is obligatory to check the person against the photograph.' On one note attached to lists of people awaiting trial for capital crimes, Stalin scribbled: 'Shoot all 138 of them.' To this, Molotov

the Ukraine. As a witness of the genocide and the famine, he sent his reports back to Britain by diplomatic pouch to elude the censor, later recalling: 'The novelty of this particular famine, what made it so diabolical, was that it was not the result of some catastrophe like a drought or an epidemic. It was the deliberate creation of a bureaucratic mind which demanded the collectivization of agriculture … without any consideration whatever of the consequences in human suffering.'

added his signature. Molotov was made Foreign Commissar on 3 May 1939 in time to negotiate non-aggression pacts with Germany (August 1939) and Japan (April 1941).

After the German invasion of the Soviet Union, he became a member of the five-man State Defence Committee responsible for the conduct of the war. The German attack had unnerved Stalin. Unable to speak to the people at the outbreak of war, he entrusted the task to Molotov. But soon Stalin's old instinct for self-preservation asserted itself. A broad hint was issued to Molotov, and when *Pravda* published his speeches, a large photo of Stalin invariably appeared alongside.

Foreign Commissar

In addition to becoming first deputy chairman of the Council of People's commissar (1941) and a member of the State Defence Committee, he negotiated mutual aid treaties with the British and the United States. At the major Allied conferences, he and Stalin were a formidable duo, Molotov appearing to be the toughest, and his leader often appearing a more moderate and subtler negotiator.

In 1949, however, Molotov fell out of favour and was removed as foreign minister. Attacks on Khrushchev, whom he denounced as 'a revisionist', hastened his downfall, and he was dismissed from office and expelled from the Communist Party. He was accused of joining the anti-party group intent on deposing Khrushchev.

The post of ambassador to Mongolia removed him from any further influence, while in 1960 he became Soviet delegate to the International Atomic Energy Agency in Vienna. Molotov and others were denounced at the 22nd Party Congress for their role in assisting Stalin in his bloody purges.

Rehabilitated during the Brezhnev years, Molotov was able to rejoin the party in 1984. Unrepentant for the past, he declared: 'There is no alternative to class struggle. The be-all and end all is not peaceful co-existence.' He died at the age of 96 in Moscow on 8 November 1986, the last of the major participants in the revolution of 1917.

At the end of 1989, just two years before the Soviet Union's final collapse, the government of Mikhail Gorbachev formally denounced as illegal the Molotov-Ribbentrop Pact. Signed on 23 August 1939, this had brought about the annexation of the Baltic States and the partition of Poland. To the end, Molotov remained unrepentant. In a rare interview, he was proud to declare: 'The fact that we survived, that socialism endured and after the war moved forward, all of this, in my opinion, is our greatest accomplishment of this period. Yes, in this achievement the epidemic of repression itself played a crucial role ... Someone had to remain untainted by all repression. So Stalin took the lead ... I was one of his chief supporters. I have no regrets over it.' Furthermore, neither had his wife. Until their last days, the couple remained passionate Stalinists.

PROTESTS

However, the OGPU could not always claim total success in their campaign of terror. Information leaked out that some of their forces were refusing to attack defenceless villages and were facing peasants armed with pitchforks and shotguns. This momentarily unnerved Stalin, who at one point believed he was facing the loss of the entire Ukraine. The whole aim of collectivization, to make agriculture and industry more efficient, was

The presence of an efficient and far-reaching rail network was vital for the success of Stalin's industrialization programme. Plans were launched to connect the Siberian and Central Asian locales, rich in natural resources, to manufacturers and consumers in the country's western areas. For this, the Turkestan-Siberian Railway, 1450km (900 miles) long, was built, using prison labour.

severely compromised. Farmers were destroying livestock, so that it should not fall into the hands of the state. An alarmingly large number of horses, vital for ploughing in the absence of tractors, was deliberately destroyed. In September 1932, Stalin introduced one of his most draconian laws: punishment by a stretch of forced labour or death for those peasants taking as much as a handful of grain or a cabbage for their own use.

Among those involved were some who acknowledged the sheer cruelty of the enterprise, at the same declaring it to be justified. A young Communist activist, Lev Kopolev, wrote: 'I saw women and children with distended bellies turning blue, with vacant lifeless eyes and corpses in ragged sheepskin coats and cheap felt-booted corpses in peasant huts, in the melted snow of old Vologda, under the bridges of Kharkov.' But in the same passage, Kopolev added: 'We were realizing historical necessity. We were performing our revolutionary duty. We were obtaining grain for the socialist fatherland.' On another occasion, he admitted: 'Scouring the countryside, searching for hidden grain … I emptied out the old folks' storage chests, stopping my ears to the children's crying and the women's wails … I was convinced I was accomplishing the great and necessary transformation of the countryside.'

Even so, there were protests from even the most loyal of party activists, including *Politburo* members, most notably in the Ukraine, where peasants were responsible for holding back the grain that Moscow was demanding. A document, headed 'Stalin and the Crisis of the Proletarian Dictatorship' was signed by a clutch of Bolsheviks, who dared to call for 'the liquidation of Stalin and his clique'. They were rounded up and deported to the camps.

Collectivization continued relentlessly. The early figure of 62 per cent of peasant households huddled into collectives had become 93 per cent by 1937. By then it was claimed that collectivization had enabled the government to feed the towns, finance the Five Year Plans and provide the workforce for industry. But it was a success that had been driven by terror, leaving a legacy of hatred for the regime among peasants, to whom it seemed that serfdom was back. With the peasantry cowed, other sections of society were next to be considered enemies: even creators of the Revolution were unsafe and could be viewed as potential rivals, ripe for destruction.

This fiercely anti-Soviet cartoon from around 1940, obviously circulated clandestinely, shows Stalin reclining in an armchair emblazoned with the hammer and sickle. The blaze of bones suggests the fate of the victims of forced labour, and above the fire hang the Soviet leader's trophy of skulls.

SOVIET INTERNMENT CAMPS

The Soviet concentration camp system had its crude beginnings in the days of the *Cheka* under the direction of the infant Bolshevik regime of July 1918, when offenders were herded into barracks, factories and even the imposing homes of dispossessed gentry. These 'class enemies' included just about anyone who could be seen as a threat to the regime. The camps, numbering some 300 at that time, were totally unsupervised and run by ill-disciplined guards, who treated their prisoners appallingly. Hunger, disease and general abuse were later reckoned to have produced mortality rates of around one-third of inmates.

Only with the cessation of the Civil War was any attempt made to centralize the prison system and to close down those early sites. The GPU/OGPU, as the successor to the *Cheka*, operated with two prisons in Moscow and Leningrad, ten small camps designed for the most dangerous prisoners, and a network of concentration camps that lay to the far north, designated as the Northern Special Purpose Camps. These were eventually to form the nucleus of the notorious Gulag and were centred on a disused monastery to the far north on the island of Solovetsky in the Arkhangel'sk province.

It was characteristic of those who controlled the OGPU that they saw the camps as providing an ideal opportunity to extend their power. They worked to persuade central government to extend the category of prisoner assigned to the camps. A significant advance was made when OGPU secured those criminals whose sentences exceeded three years. All were forced into undertaking hard labour – originally seen as playing their part in fulfilling what were regarded as the economic goals of socialism.

A major reform came on 7 April 1930 with the formation of the Main Administration of Corrective Labour Camps and Labour Settlements, whose original cumbersome acronym GUITLTP became Gulag, or Main Administration of Camps. This was headed by two OGPU officials, Lazar Kogan and Matvei Berman, the latter destined to take over the entire Gulag at the age of 35.

By then, the emphasis had shifted from socialist ideology to strictly economic considerations. Menzhinsky and Yagoda, the two senior officials chiefly involved, decreed that the camps should provide a labour pool for the construction and maintenance of mines in the far north. Mining and logging were among the most common of activities carried out by prisoners in the Gulags. The extent of the harshness can be gauged from the fact that, in a Gulag mine, an individual's production quota might be as high as 13,000kg (29,000lbs) of ore per day. Failure by an inmate to meet these targets resulted in a loss of rations and the inevitable effect on health. Malnutrition was not the only consequence. Inmates were forced to work in inhuman conditions with their captors paying little or no regard to the brutal climate. There was scarcely ever adequate clothing, food or medical treatment. Nor were there any means available to combat the lack of vitamins, resulting in nutritional diseases such as scurvy. In many camps, the guards fared little better. They had every interest in keeping the inmates in line. If a prisoner escaped on a guard's watch, the guard could be stripped of his uniform to became a prisoner himself. One of the chief projects undertaken was the construction of the 227km (141 mile) long White Sea Canal, dug to the north of present-day St Petersburg. An estimated 128,000 to 180,000 convicts were made to dig the canal with their own hands, digging in large part through granite. Labour, amassed by Yagoda's cohorts, was supplied by a mix of peasants, political prisoners and convicts stationed in nine camps along the route. Even the engineers were OGPU prisoners. The cost in prisoners' lives was put at 10,000. For

Yagoda it was a personal triumph: the canal was built under budget in less than two years. The effect on the labourers was of no consequence: Stalin had been given proof positive of the OGPU's benefit to the economy.

The Great Terror

By the summer of 1934, when the NKVD replaced the OGPU and took over unified control of the entire security and prison system, the Gulag embodied a string of camps. This included the Far-Eastern Construction Administration, a network in eastern Siberia, which mined the world's largest deposits of gold in one of the world's least habitable regions.

Some three years later, when Stalin's Great Terror with its multiple purges was underway, literally hundreds of thousands of individuals were arrested and sentenced to long prison terms in camps for various forms of 'counter-revolutionary activities'. The number of executions has been put overall at 800,000. During World War II, particularly on the occasions of triumphs such as the battles of Stalingrad and Kursk, the full resources of Soviet propaganda were marshaled to proclaim the achievements of 'our glorious Red Army', which told only part of the story. The Gulag populations had declined sharply, owing to the mass release of countless prisoners, who were conscripted and sent directly to fight in the front lines, often into penal battalions.

With the coming of peace, the number of inmates in prison camps and colonies again rose sharply, reaching approximately 2.5 million by the early 1950s. While some of these were deserters and war criminals, there were also repatriated Soviet prisoners of war and others accused of treason and 'cooperation with an enemy'. Large numbers of civilians from the Soviet territories that had been occupied, as well as from the territories annexed

by the Soviet Union after the war, were also sent there. Even survivors of Nazi concentration camps were transported directly to Soviet ones on the grounds that, since they had survived the war, they must somehow have collaborated with the enemy. A number of the German camps were taken over virtually intact: surviving Nazi emblems were torn down and replaced with Soviet ones.

The state continued to maintain the camp system for a while after Stalin's death in March 1953. The release of political prisoners started in the following year and became widespread, together with the rehabilitation of many found guilty of the worst crimes of treason. The rush to disassociate the Soviet Union from its Stalinist past was accelerated by Nikita Khrushchev's denunciation of Stalinism at the 20th Congress of the Communist Party of the Soviet Union in February 1956. By the end of the 1950s, virtually all 'corrective labour camps' had ceased to exist. Nonetheless, several camps located in Soviet satellites such as Czechoslovakia, Poland and Mongolia remained.

Nearly four decades of Soviet history were spanned by the Gulag. The cultural impact remains enormous, most notably in literature with the work of Alexander Solzhenitsyn (b. 1918). His first book, *One Day In The Life of Ivan Denisovich*, was centred around a typical day of the Gulag inmate, demonstrating the extent of governmental repression against its own citizens. This was followed by *The Gulag Archipelago* which, along with all his writings and those of others, did not hesitate to chastise the Soviet people for their tolerance and apathy regarding the Gulag. But he paid tribute, too, to the courage and resolve of those who had been incarcerated.

In 1991, the Russian parliament passed the 'Declaration of Rights and Freedoms of the Individual' which sought to uphold the individual's entitlement to disagree with the government.

CHAPTER 4

A HIGHLY CONVENIENT MURDER

A ready-made pretext for a wholesale purge of Stalin's potential rivals was afforded by the murder of his outspoken critic Sergei Kirov. Among the most prominent victims to follow was Leon Trotsky, designated an 'Enemy of the People'.

With the removal of Menzhinsky, Genrikh Yagoda's career seemed assured. But while the OGPU had proved effective in rounding up kulaks and in the creation of labour camps and colonies, there were those who felt it lacked sufficient power to deal with threats nearer home. An infinitely more effective instrument of repression, efficient and centralized, emerged with the NKVD (*Narodnyi Kommissariat Vnutrennikh Del* – Commissariat for Internal Affairs) as the replacement for the OGPU.

A wise opportunist, Yagoda hastened to prove his loyalty to Stalin by frantic empire-building. The ordinary police or militia became unified under the NKVD, along with the creation of Special Sessions to judge the full range of counter-revolutionary and terrorist crimes. Inquisitors were not required to call witnesses and those accused were barred from doing so. Stalin's suspicion of intrigues, real or imagined, became inflamed by the actions of Martemyan Ryutin. A candidate member of the Central Committee, he criticized the harsh methods of collectivization, supported by other minor party officials, some of whom were adherents of Bukharin. This led to Ryutin's expulsion from the party and a sharp warning from the OGPU. It failed to silence him. Then followed the so-called Ryutin Platform, a document calling for a reduction of investment in heavy industry and the liberalization of the condition of the peasantry. Furthermore, Ryutin

Opposite: On 7 December 1930, at the climax of the Moscow trial for treason of members of the Industrial Party, the verdict is read to a crowded courtroom. Technocrats and engineers accused of planning to overthrow the Soviet Union had been rounded up by the OGPU. Many of the subsequent death sentences were commuted because the accused had the specialist knowledge Stalin needed to implement his upcoming Five Year Plan.

condemned Stalin as 'the evil genius of the Russian Revolution' for encouraging lawlessness and terror in the countryside, while reducing the press 'to a monstrous factory of lies'. Finally, the Platform stated: 'Stalin and his clique will not and cannot voluntarily give up their position, so they must be removed by force.'

THE MURDER OF KIROV

Ryutin also demanded that Trotsky be readmitted to the Party. Stalin, in the grips of one of his periodic bouts of paranoia and anticipating an attempt on his own life, appealed to the *Politburo* to sanction Ryutin's execution as a traitor, but his plea was rejected. Then came a further blow. Prominent among those who argued against the death penalty was Sergei Kostrikov (1886–1934), a former journalist who had chosen the name Kirov as his Bolshevik pseudonym. A persuasive speaker and Congress member, he flourished under Stalin, leading to membership of the *Politburo,* and appointment as secretary to both the Central Committee and the party in Leningrad, where he had been charged to root out Left opposition. He was a few years younger than his chief, who treated him like a brother. The pair often took their holidays together. Indeed, they were thought to be so close that many felt Kirov was being groomed for the future leadership of the party. In the manner of so many others who failed to sense the danger of becoming too close to Stalin, Kirov overreached himself. Suspicions were aroused, particularly when it became evident that he was taking increasingly independent lines at *Politburo* meetings. Furthermore, his weakness for drink made him garrulous and on occasions bluntly critical of his mentor. A further source of irritation was his insistence at Congress meetings that he should sit not on the stage but with his own Leningrad delegation, a pose that was interpreted by his critics as a blatant snub.

In a bid to keep his protégé in line, Stalin insisted during the summer of 1934 that the two of them went for a prolonged break to his dacha. During it, he made strenuous efforts to persuade Kirov to change jobs and go to work in Moscow. Kirov refused and returned to Leningrad and to his party headquarters in the Smolny Institute. Over the succeeding months, Stalin insisted on seeing Kirov regularly to keep tabs on him, loading him with assignments from Moscow. Then at 4.30 p.m. on 1 December, while making his way to his office, Kirov was shot in the neck at close range. The assassin was Leonid Nikolaev, a deranged party member to whom Kirov had refused to give a job. He then attempted to turn the weapon on himself but was dragged away and later executed.

THE PURGES BEGIN

Stalin's reaction was to speed by train to Leningrad, drafting a decree to deal with 'terrorists' and placing the NKVD at the centre of events. Part of

the decree read: 'The case of those accused of preparing or committing terrorist acts is to be dealt with in an accelerated way; judicial organs may not hold up the carrying out of death sentences because of appeals for mercy from criminals of this category. The organs of the NKVD are to carry out death sentences passed on criminals of the above categories as soon as the court has pronounced sentence'.

Later, however, Stalin considered that the draft needed strengthening and declared:

'1. The investigation of such cases must be completed in no more than ten days.

2. The charges will be handed to the accused 24 hours before the court examines the case.

3. The case will be heard with no participation by other parties.

4. No appeals for quashing the verdict or for mercy will be allowed.

5. The death sentence is to be carried out as soon as it has been pronounced.'

Historians are still divided as to whether Stalin himself arranged the murder of a known rival. Many have wondered why Kirov's regular bodyguards were

After denouncing the 'evil murder of Comrade Kirov', Stalin (far right) leads Kirov's funeral procession in Moscow during December 1934. With him are key members of the government. On Stalin's right is Klementi Voroshilov and, behind, Yacheslav Molotov, Lazar Kaganovich and Andrei Zhdanov.

not present at the time of the murder. Others hazard that the deranged Nikolaev, spurned on by hatred of Kirov, acted alone, arguing that Stalin and Yagoda, if responsible, could have called on the droves of professional killers they had at their disposal.

Whatever the truth, Kirov's death could scarcely have been more advantageous to Stalin, who had been handed a ready-made pretext for the purge of rivals. No time was wasted in targeting a likely master planner who could have manipulated Nikolaev – Stalin's old rival, Trotsky. The *Politburo* was called on to give support for what amounted to a purge of the party; predictably, a majority agreed. Any possibility of achieving reconciliation between the various groups in the *Politburo* and party was now at an end. Driven by the new powers of the NKVD, the Revolution proceeded to devour its own creators.

Those rounded up were herded either into police vans or into less conspicuous vehicles, so as not to alert the victims in advance or to disturb the neighbourhood. They were rushed to the headquarters of the State Security Division, a grim building in Lubyanka Square, soon the most feared building in Moscow. The detested Trotsky, living at the time in exile on the small island of Prinkipo, near the Turkish border, was not accessible, but supporters like Zinoviev and Kamenev were arrested and put on trial, accused of taking instructions from Trotsky for the murder of Kirov and the planned assassination of Stalin and other party leaders. They were among some 300 taken in for questioning, before which they were kept in windowless cells under strong electric light that was never extinguished.

The Industrial Party trial of 1930 – the first of many – was an elaborately staged affair. The existence of plentiful evidence against the accused was inferred by the mountain of files being carried into court.

Guards forced them to stand for hours to ensure that they got no sleep. Along with lack of food, this kept them tired and exhausted, unable to think clearly and eventually prepared to confess to just about anything, particularly crimes that were high on the NKVD's investigative agenda. Invariably subjected to slander and abuse, they were also persuaded to give details of crimes allegedly committed by friends. These confessions were also shown to other prisoners in a bid to persuade them to make admissions of guilt. Torture, although not officially sanctioned in the early stages of the purges, was also used. If faced with a blank refusal to co-operate, families, including children, were arrested and used as an added inducement. When all else failed, prisoners were offered a deal: sign an agreement to confess, and a death penalty would be avoided; refuse, and execution would be without trial. In most cases, it made little difference: once the confessions were secured, executions were carried out anyway.

THE SHOW TRIALS

With the intention of creating a strong sense of fear throughout the Soviet Union and her satellites, three major 'show trials' were held, in fulfilment of orders to the NKVD to 'put an end once and for all to the foul subversive work against the foundations of the Soviet state'. The first, the trial of the

Throughout the Industrial Party trial, a vituperative campaign was launched against those in the dock, seen here. The trial was held in the full glare of the media. Giant spotlights were used for the cameras, while speeches for defence and prosecution were broadcast. The KGB later claimed the existence of an 'underground espionage centre… directed and financed by Western secret agents'.

two 'leading Left' deviationists, Zinoviev and Kamenev, who had been induced to confess their crimes, took place in the October Hall of the Trade Union Building in Moscow. Flanked by NKVD guards with fixed bayonets, the accused, including 14 other defendants, were totally demoralized. The four articles of the indictment included charges that 'During the period from

ANDREI VYSHINSKY

Andrei Yanuarievich Vyshinsky, Procurator General and Chief Prosecutor, was a notorious figure in the succession of Soviet treason trials. He was notorious for his invective in terrorizing prisoners who had already been cowed by torture, sleeplessness and threats to their families and who were in no state to mount any form of defence.

Born in 1883, the son of a affluent noble family in Odessa, Vyshinsky had a background that was conventional enough but scarcely an ideal prescription for survival in a Russia gripped by civil war between 1918 and 1920. He studied at the University of Kiev, joined the Menshevik (literally 'minority') branch of the Social Democratic party and fought in the Bolshevik ranks. From then on it was a straight career rise – Professor of Law and later rector at the University of Moscow, followed in 1933 by the post of deputy state prosecutor. As chief prosecutor, he laid out two precepts as the legal cornerstone for treason trials: 'Criminal law is a tool of the class struggle' and 'Confession is a queen over all sorts of evidence'. Both precepts were later embodied in a monograph, *Theory of Judicial Proofs*, which gained him the Stalin Prize in 1947.

Possessed of abundant energy, but battling constantly with bouts of eczema, he possessed an actor's gift when it came to vituperation. This was particularly notable during the trials of the 'terrorists' Zinoviev and Kamenev, together with fourteen others, for alleged involvement in the murder of Kirov. In his closing speech he declared: 'The enemy is cunning. A cunning enemy must not

be spared. The whole people rose to its feet as soon as these ghastly crimes became known ... I want to conclude by reminding you, comrade judges, of those demands which the law makes in cases of the gravest crimes against the state. I take the liberty of reminding you that it is your duty, once you find these people, all sixteen of them, guilty of crimes against the state, to apply to them in full measure those articles of the law which have been preferred against them by the prosecution. I demand that dogs gone mad should be shot – every one of them'. Enthusiastic for what was officially called the 'Highest Measure of Punishment' and by virtue of his office expected to attend executions, he nonetheless usually declined, due to an unfortunate squeamishness.

The end of World War II and the advent of the Cold War saw no diminution in Vyshinsky's ruthlessness. In 1945, following the decision at the Yalta Conference to hand over 90 per cent of Romania to Stalin, he engineered the enforced resignation of the country's King Michael. Protests to him by the king were greeted with the sneer: '*I am Yalta*'.

In March 1949, Vyshinsky became foreign minister and, representing the Soviet Union at the United Nations, frequently launched bitter verbal attacks on the United States during the Korean War. He was demoted to first deputy foreign minister after Stalin's death in 1953, but remained the permanent Soviet representative at the United Nations. He died from a massive heart attack in New York in 1954.

1932 to 1936 a joint Trotskyist-Zinovievist Centre was organized in Moscow which set itself the task of carrying out a number of acts of terror against the leaders of the Communist Party of the Soviet Union (Bolsheviks) in order to arrogate power to itself … That one of these terrorist groups, which was operating under the direct instructions of Zinoviev and Trotsky as well as those of the Joint Trotskyist Centre … perpetrated the despicable murder of Comrade S M Kirov …' The outlining of the prosecution's case took several hours, at which point, the General State Prosecutor, Andrei Vyshinsky (1883–1954), ranted: 'I declare that these dogs who have gone mad should all be shot.' At the end of his own speech, Vyshinsky condemned the accused as 'liars and clowns, miserable pygmies, lapdogs and yappers'.

The foreign press had been admitted to the trial and was at first bewildered to hear the defendants confessing to plotting the death of Kirov and Stalin, and allegations that the absent Trotsky was being influenced by Germany to impose a fascist dictatorship on the Soviet people. There was cynical disbelief that left-wing Bolsheviks could inexplicably become right-wing extremists virtually overnight, but it could not be denied that they had openly confessed in court. As one observer noted: 'All defendants seemed eager to heap accusation upon accusation upon themselves. They required little cross-examination by the prosecutor'. Indeed, their confessions had been positively cringing, with Kamenev declaring: 'No matter what my sentence will be, I consider it just'. With the delivery of the pre-decided verdict, one of the prisoners shouted: 'Long live the cause of Marx, Engels, Lenin and Stalin!' The executions of Zinoviev and Kamenev by shots to the back of the head followed swiftly.

The Zinoviev/Kamenev trial of 1936 was followed by another at the start of the following year, centring on 17 major figures who were accused of conspiring with Germany and Japan to overthrow the Soviet government. The third trial followed the arrest of Bukharin, who had managed to rehabilitate himself somewhat, playing a large part in the drafting of a remodelled Soviet Constitution in 1936 and becoming the editor of the official government newspaper *Izvestia*. Given no part in active politics, he was increasingly aware that his earlier reservations about Stalin would not be forgotten and became resigned to living on borrowed time, contenting himself with condemning in print what he considered to be the Soviet Union's conciliatory

Andrei Vyshinsky, dapper and primly bespectacled, caught in a misleadingly calm pose in court. At Stalin's behest, he did not shrink from verbal bullying of defendants, none of whom were a match for his hectoring, withering sarcasm.

Nikolai Ivanovitch Yezhov, pictured here in Moscow in 1937, was the first ethnic Russian to head the NKVD, with the title of People's Commissar of Internal Affairs. Within the Party apparatus, he created a security wing that many historians believe helped to plan the murder of Kirov. A heavy drinker well on the way to becoming an alcoholic, he was known to attend torture sessions and executions when drunk.

relations with Nazi Germany. But Stalin had already dubbed him a Trotskyite. He was expelled from the party and arrested. Among the grotesque allegations were charges of seeking to enlist in foreign intelligence services and plotting to assassinate Lenin and Stalin. During Bukharin's examination, observers in the courtroom, almost certainly planted by the NKVD, chorused 'Swine!' and 'Liar'.

Another of the defendants was Nicholas Krestinsky, a veteran Bolshevik who had been elected to the Central Committee in August 1917 and to the first Politburo two years later. At first, he had given his support to Trotsky during the latter's bitter dispute over the direction of the country, but later was canny enough to withdraw it, switching to a career in diplomacy, which included becoming Soviet Ambassador to Germany. The mere fact that he had been an ally of Trotsky, however, was enough to ensure his arrest and he was also accused of traitorous association with the German secret service.

Protests against the charges were rare during the trials, but Krestinsky proved an exception, declaring to the presiding judge Vasili Ulrikh: 'I do not recognize that I am guilty. I am not a Trotskyite. I was never a member of the right-winger and Trotskyite bloc, which I did not know to exist. Nor have I committed a single one of the crimes imputed to me personally and in particular I am not guilty of having maintained relations with the German intelligence service'. It did not take long for cohorts of the NKVD to persuade him otherwise.

The next day, Krestinsky, looking pale and drawn and clearly a broken man, made a total reversal of his position, apologizing to the court and stating: 'Yesterday, under the influence of a momentary keen feeling of false shame, evoked by the atmosphere of the dock and the painful impression created by the public reading of the indictment, which was aggravated by my poor health, I could not bring myself to tell the truth. I could not bring myself to say that I was guilty. And instead of saying, "Yes, I am guilty" I almost mechanically answered, "No, I am not guilty".' On 15 March 1938, the Soviet government announced that the death sentences of all 17, including Krestinsky, had been carried out. According to witnesses, Bukharin and a fellow prisoner Alexei Rykov, a member of the Politburo, faced their executioners cursing Stalin.

Swept up also in the assorted recriminations was Yagoda himself, accused of incompetence in safeguarding the life of Kirov and for not pressing the case against Bukharin with sufficient zeal. Brought to trial, he admitted poisoning his predecessor Menzhinsky (among others) and attempting to poison his successor Yezhov with mercury vapour, and to having expressed sympathy with Bukharin. For good measure, he also confessed to working for the German, Japanese and Polish intelligence services. Under interrogation, he had been physically assaulted and had cut a pathetic figure, his hands handcuffed behind his back, his trousers falling down. His execution, following a fruitless plea to be allowed to work as a labourer, was followed by savage recriminations against his family, including his wife Lili, who was sentenced to eight years in the camps and condemned to death a year later.

> 'Death solves all problems – no man, no problem.'
>
> —attributed to Stalin

'THE DWARF'

His successor, Nikolai Yezhov (1895–1940), who had intrigued against his predecessor and had already gained the ear of Stalin, exhibited a frenzied enthusiasm for arrest and torture. Only 1.5m (5 ft) tall and crippled, he was known as 'The Dwarf'. Barely educated beyond an elementary level, he initially fostered the image of a party hack, working the political system in various regional committees of the Communist Party. He was possessed of considerable charm when he wished to use it, and his career moves worked well: at the start of 1935, he became Chairman of the Central Committee for Party Control. This enabled him to gain Stalin's favour as a dedicated loyalist and at the same time to enhance his own future by preparing a paper which became in part the ideological basis for the forthcoming purges, arguing that political opposition must inevitably lead to violence and terrorism. Above all, the paper helped him achieve his ultimate goal of becoming head of the NKVD, whose recent achievements he criticized, arguing that the main thrust of the operations of state security were directed 'not against organized counter-revolutionary organizations but chiefly against isolated incidents of anti-Soviet agitations, against every sort of malfeasance in office, hooliganism, ordinary crimes and so on'. An additional criticism was made of the special prisons for political detainees, which 'resembled forced vacation homes rather than prisons … Inmates were afforded the opportunity of associating closely with each other, of discussing all political matters taking place in the country, of working out plans for anti-Soviet operations to be carried out by their organizations, and of maintaining relationships with people on the outside'.

As head of the NKVD and a member of the Presidium Central Executive Committee, he enjoyed for some time after Yagoda's dismissal the full trust

To ensure the loyalty of his workforce, Stalin was keen that it should be kept informed of all measures to ensure state security. On 28 August 1936, turbine shop workers in Leningrad listened to reports on the trial and execution of Zinoviev, Kamenev and 14 others convicted of allegedly plotting against Stalin and of complicity in Kirov's murder. Workers countrywide were persuaded to pass resolutions approving of the government's action.

of Stalin, to whom he was ordered to report directly and in secret. His main remit was to arrest and eliminate doubtful members of the Soviet political and military establishment, together with others suspected of disloyalty and 'wrecking'.

The initial purges were of surviving gentry and *petit bourgeois* whom Yagoda had placed in senior positions. Those who were spared the bullet were sent to the Gulag, which Yezhov considered was under-used. Surviving figures for 1938 revealed that deaths among the chaotic and overcrowded camps soared to 90,000, representing 10 per cent of inmates. Nocturnal crime on the streets of cities, particularly Moscow and Leningrad, reached an all-time high.

Previous Communist propaganda tended to catergorise common criminals as redeemable brothers of the working class. Such rhetoric was now discarded; those arrested were deported and executed. The NKVD's agents were literally everywhere, having benefited from close study of the practices of Hitler's *Gestapo:* an anti-Soviet joke uttered in a bar could lead to arrest under a catch-all article of the Soviet criminal code. Condemning

'propaganda and group activity', it meant just about anything that the NKVD decreed. Yezhov pushed the NKVD into overdrive, quadrupling the number of detectives employed and recruiting extra staff to beat out confessions. The executions he decreed were carried out,not in the cellars of the Lubyanka, but in an abattoir that had been constructed in an adjacent courtyard. Its far wall was built of logs to absorb any bullets while hoses washed away fluids. After the shootings, the corpses were put into metal boxes and driven to one of a number of crematoria. The ashes were subsequently scattered in mass graves.

BERIA – THE SOVIET HIMMLER

By late 1938, Stalin considered that the terror, for a time at least, had run its course and that the high number of executions was denting morale and efficiency. With such a heavy self-imposed workload, Yezhov's health, never robust, went into decline and his drinking worsened. That November, he was dismissed. His successor, the Georgian Lavrenti Beria (1899–1953), had originally trained as an architect in Baku, but had been attracted by the

Cheka. This he had served with dedication, eventually becoming OGPU chief for the Transcaucasus, where he carried out a series of purges.

From the very start of his career, Beria had been heartily disliked by all. He was balding, short, and fleshy, with sensual lips and snakelike eyes glistening behind his professorial pince-nez, and his sexual proclivities were both perverted and insatiable. His habit was to prowl the streets in his official limousine on the lookout for a young woman. When a suitable one was spotted, the driver was ordered to stop, seize her and throw her in the

THE PURGES OF THE ARMED FORCES

During the course of the purges of the 1930s, Mikhail Shpigelglaz, head of the NKVD's foreign intelligence section, learned of a conspiracy aimed at nothing less than the overthrow of Stalin and the Soviet Union, engineered by factions within the Red Army. Senior commanders were swiftly placed under round-the-clock surveillance. Yezhov particularly singled out Marshal of the Soviet Union Mikhail Nikolaievich Tukhachevsky (1893–1937), who was accused of being 'politically contaminated'. Predictably, no time was wasted in alerting Stalin. Soviet officers were rounded up for the usual brutal interrogations: under torture, a brigade commander confessed to the existence of an army plot.

It was not the first time that Tukhachevsky, a gifted, dashing aristocrat, had been in trouble. Born near Smolensk into a family of Polish origin, he had joined the Bolsheviks after the Russian Revolution. His rapid rise within the Red Army meant that during the Russian Civil War he was responsible for defending Moscow. Trotsky, then Bolshevik Defence Commissar, appointed him to the command of the 5th Army in 1919 and he led the campaign to recapture Siberia from Whites. The next year he headed the Bolshevik armies during the Polish–Soviet War, but was defeated outside Warsaw and had to suffer accusations of having 'grandiose plans' and being over-ambitious and 'counter-revolutionary'.

But despite making enemies among junior

officers who resented his ill-concealed arrogance, Tukhachevsky went on to serve as Chief of Staff and Deputy Commissar for Defence and in 1931 had a leading role in key reforms of the Red Army. But his time was running out. Although surviving accounts by Russian and German researchers differ, matters seemingly were brought to a head in the winter of 1936.

Nazi Espionage

The man responsible was General Nikolai Skoblin, a Paris-based Russian émigré, who pursued a precarious existence spying both for the Soviet NKVD and for the Nazi SD. In a meeting with Reinhard Heydrich (1904–42), the SD supremo, Skoblin claimed that Tukhachevsky was not only planning a coup against the Red Army but was also intent on raising contingents of it against the Third Reich.

To Heydrich and to Heinrich Himmler (1900–45), head of the SS, the potential value of Skoblin's information was obvious. If Stalin was informed that a *putsch* was in the offing, the elimination of some of his senior military leaders would make Soviet forces a lot less dangerous for Germany.

But rumours would not be enough. It was plain to Heydrich, backed by Hitler, that Stalin would require proof of treason. If such proof did not exist, it would have to be supplied; the obvious mechanism was forgery. The production of counterfeit material – bogus correspondence back of the car. She was then driven off to a quiet spot, where Beria raped her. Who dared complain?

To Stalin, Beria's fawning sycophancy was a source of constant irritation, but his peerless energy and organizational skills were too valuable to ignore. Beria received the leader's imprimatur: 'Lavrenti Beria is our Himmler.' One of Beria's priorities on succeeding to the NKVD was to be rid of Yezhov, whom he had constantly undermined by drip-feeding insinuations direct to Stalin. Even so, Yezhov was kept on ice until 16 January 1940, when Stalin

between officers of the German and Soviet armies as well as skillful forgeries of Tukhachevsky's signature – presented no problems for the SD. The results reached Stalin via the NKVD.

Heydrich's SD could claim the success for having exposed Tukhachevsky's intentions via General Skoblin. However, the British Soviet affairs specialist Robert Conquest believes that Stalin had intended all along to deal with the army and had welcomed the additional 'proof' presented to him. The aim was to eliminate a swathe of senior personnel, some of whom were deemed especially dangerous since they had served in Tsarist times.

Ironically, Stalin decided not to make use of the forged letters, preferring the well-tried methods of intimidation, extracting confessions, torture and blackmail. In any case, ahead of Heydrich, Yezhov had set up an 'Administration for Special Tasks'. Known as 'The Special Bureau', this had undertaken the investigations against Tukhachevsky.

Round-ups and Interrogations

By 3 March 1937, the ground had been laid. On that day, Stalin, in a speech of heavy hints to the Central Committee of the Communist Party, referred to the enormous damage 'which a handful of spies in the Red Army could do to the country'. On 11 May, Tukhachevsky lost his job as Deputy Commissar for War and faced demotion to Commander of the Volga Military District. He was

arrested three days later, along with seven others deemed to be his co-conspirators. Their fate followed a predictable pattern: interrogations, sleep deprivation and round-the-clock beatings with heavy truncheons; Tukhachevsky signed his confession with a hand that streamed blood. Following the trial, all eight were led off one by one to be shot by V.M. Blokhin, the Lubyanka's chief executioner.

With the advent of Beria, the brutality of interrogations surpassed anything that had gone before. A typical example was that of Marshal Vasily Blyukher, a former factory worker who had built up Russia's defences against Japan with conspicuous success. He had been arrested for being, among other things, a Japanese spy. Dying on 9 November 1938, he was already blinded in one eye, had suffered a blood clot in the lung and his abdominal organs had been beaten to pulp. But Stalin's thirst for revenge was not slaked. On his instructions, orders were sent out to all the republics, ordering workers, peasants and soldiers to demand capital sentences.

Statistics differ on the numbers from the armed forces wiped out in the purges, but it has been reckoned that between May 1937 and the following September, some 36,700 army officers and over 3000 naval officers were dismissed. A total for 1937–41 of 43,000 officers at battalion and company level were arrested and either shot or sent to the Gulag.

signed his death sentence among 345 others. On 2 February, after being incarcerated in a drying-out clinic and being maltreated by the very same people who but a short time had been his subordinates, he faced Ulrikh, the hanging judge. Previously, he had spurned a suggestion from Beria that he should confess, declaring that during 25 years serving the party he had 'fought honourably against enemies and exterminated them … Used everything at my disposal to expose conspiracies'. Calm at this point, he made his last statement, contradicting the plea of guilty which he had been forced to make, merely requesting, 'Shoot me quietly, without putting me through any agony'. His courage failed him, though, when the sentence was pronounced. He was dragged screaming to his own execution yard and shot.

Ordinary Russians, disturbed and bewildered by accounts of the widely publicized purges, were relieved by the advent of Beria, portrayed for public consumption as an avuncular reformer. He was swift to sense that the NKVD, which had exercised virtually unlimited power under Yezhov, was in urgent need of reform. There was a general feeling that the terror had run its course and that arrests on the flimsiest of charges were a waste of manpower and also counter-productive. Conventional methods of police procedure were introduced: public trials could be held only where there was solid evidence of terrorist crimes being either anticipated or committed. Surveillance became precisely that: no longer simply a euphemism for arrest followed by intimidation and execution.

Although Laventri Beria was one of the most ruthless leaders in the Soviet administration as leader of the NKVD, attempts were made, following the programme of purges, to portray him as a comparatively liberal reformer. In fact, under his leadership, arrests and execution continued, as they had under Yezhov. In March 2000, the Russian Federation Supreme court refused an application by members of Beria's family to overturn his 1953 conviction.

THE ASSASSINATION OF TROTSKY

As a result of these changes, arrests were stepped up. A notable instance was that of a veteran Bolshevik, close associate and fellow Georgian, Grigory Ordzhonikidze (1886–1937). A *Politburo* member, he had served as chairman of the Workers and Peasants Inspectorate, supporting the campaign against the kulaks. But later he had objected forcibly to some of the trials of officials. Stalin had previously hailed him 'the perfect Bolshevik', but he was now denounced for 'hooliganism'. Furthermore, he was suspected of using his influence to protect associates under investigation by the NKVD and his apartment was raided for incriminating evidence. Rumours spread that he was preparing to denounce Stalin in a speech at the April 1937 Plenum. Two months before the Plenum, Ordzhonikidze was dead. A hastily issued medical bulletin stated: 'At 17.30, while he was having his afternoon rest, he suddenly felt ill and a few minutes later died of paralysis of the heart'. This alleged cause of death was suspiciously convenient. In fact, it was a plain lie. A shot had rung out in the family apartment and Ordzhonikidze had been found dead on his bed. On receiving news of the killing, Stalin hastened to view the body, at the same time ensuring that the event afforded a photo opportunity by assembling Ordzhonikidze's widow Zinaida and suitably shocked associates for the camera.

The death was widely assumed to be suicide, but doubts persisted and it was suggested later that this had been an assassination staged by the NKVD to look like suicide. Whatever the truth, Ordzhonikidze was hailed as a Stalinist for public consumption and provided with an elaborate lying-in-state and funeral, his ashes buried near those of Kirov in the Kremlin wall.

Before and during World War II, Beria enjoyed the freedom to do virtually what he wanted. There was, however, one piece of pressing and unfinished business from the purge: the elimination of Leo Trotsky, now known to be living in exile in Mexico. Assassinations were not confined to the Soviet Union; the tentacles of the security service were extending widely. The headless body of Trotsky's former secretary, Rudolf Klement, was fished out of the Seine in 1937, while another associate, who had sought refuge in Switzerland, was lured to a Lausanne cafe, shot and beaten to death.

The room in Coyoacan, Mexico, where Leon Trotsky was struck down with a cut-down ice pick concealed by Ramon Mercader under his raincoat. The Spanish Communist worked in league with the NKVD, which favoured this method for despatching its victims.

From the moment of his arrival in Mexico, the local Communist party slavishly followed the Moscow line, seeking to discredit Trotsky in every way possible. Newspapers and journals combined with the party-controlled trade union federation to launch a campaign of allegations that he was plotting against the government and 'collaborating with fascist and reactionary elements'. The first direct attempt on Trotsky's life came at midnight on 24 May 1940. The NKVD went to elaborate lengths to outfit a death squad with bogus police and army uniforms. In addition, the men carried a full armoury of sub-machine guns, home-made incendiary devices and two dynamite bombs. They also had ladders, grappling hooks and a power saw. Once inside, they raked the apartment with machine-gun fire and set off the incendiaries, intending not only to kill but to destroy Trotsky's considerable archives. Trotsky and his wife Natalia survived by lying under a bed, while their grandson Seva was slightly injured. For good measure, a time bomb was left behind by the departing raiders, but it failed to explode. A security guard, who had been tricked into admitting the gang, was dragged away and later killed, his corpse tossed into a lime pit.

Leon Trotsky on his death bed. Before he died, he pointed to his heart, gasping in English: 'I feel here…that this is the end… This time they've succeeded.'

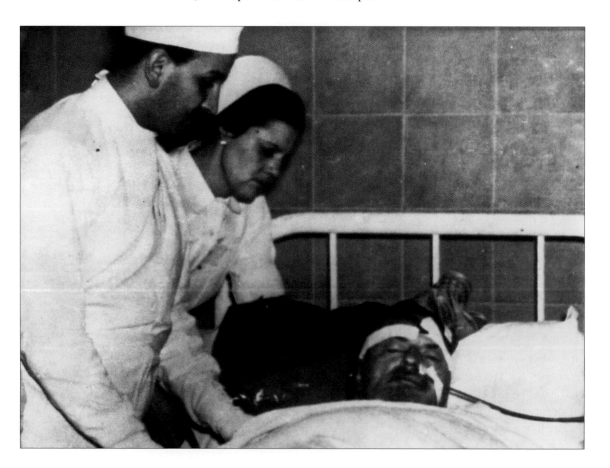

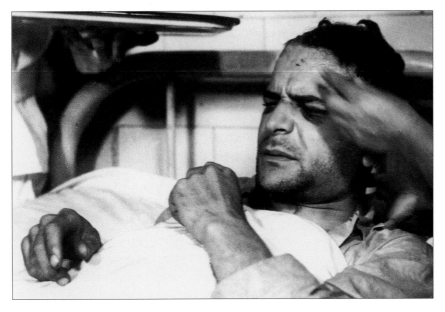

Ramon Mercader pictured in hospital in Mexico City on 20 August 1940. His NKVD connection was not released until the fall of the Soviet Union. Released on 6 May 1960, he moved to Havana under the protection of Fidel Castro. The next year he was awarded the Hero of the Soviet Union medal. He died back in Havana in 1978, achieving a place of honour in Moscow's KGB museum.

Planning for the next attempt was in the hands of Naum Eitingen, an NKVD agent. He recruited Ramon Mercader, a fanatical Stalinist, ordering him to gain Trotsky's confidence, enter his house and kill him. After some informal meetings between the two, Mercader asked Trotsky to read an article the other man was writing. This gave Mercader, armed with a concealed ice pick, the chance he was seeking. The weapon was brought down with considerable force on Trotsky's skull, but the blow was not enough to kill him and his screams alerted his guards, who rushed into the study. The assault on Mercader was stopped by the intervention of Trotsky himself, who yelled: 'Do not kill him. The man has a story to tell.' Trotsky was rushed to an emergency hospital, where he died 24 hours later. Mercader, himself in hospital following the severe beating he had received, readily confessed to the killing. Posing for photographs, he also demonstrated how he had used the ice pick. He was sentenced to 20 years for the murder. A key chapter of the purges was closed.

At the same time, a significant reformation of the NKVD was underway, dictated by the advent of war. The need for further strengthening of the security services was deemed a priority. Thus a law of 3 February 1941 took the Chief Office of State Security out of the NKVD, turning that office into an independent ministry or People's Commissariat, NKGB (*Narodnyi Kommissariat Gozudarstvennoi Bezopastnosti*). In charge was Vsevolod Nikolayevich Merkulov (1895–63), an old crony of Beria, who had served as his deputy in the Caucasus. The power base of the NKGB expanded rapidly and included responsibility for supervision of the Red Army and Navy. The entire security apparatus was now geared for war.

CHAPTER 5

DEPORTATIONS AT DAYBREAK

Under the shadow of war and possible threats to his borders and his rule, Stalin embarked on ruthless deportation of millions of potential enemies, including Crimean Tartars, Ukrainians, Poles, Latvians, Greeks and Turks.

Aside from the increasingly strident nationalism of Nazi Germany, the rulers of Soviet Russia throughout the 1930s perceived danger lying to the east, west and south of its borders. Finland, Poland, the Japanese Empire and the vast spread of Baltic states were deemed hostile. As a deliberate policy, more than 1.5 million people, Muslims, Volga Germans and seven nationalities from the Crimea and the Caucasus were forcibly deported and resettled. Pretexts, when they were given at all, were a suspected resistance to Soviet rule, a desire for separatism and, with the advent of war, alleged collaboration with the Germans.

The hyper-efficient machinery of deportation came into the hands of Beria, the NKVD chief, who prowled the Caucasus and Ukraine in his special train, selecting Crimean Tartars, Kalmyks and Chechens for particularly vicious ethnic cleansing. The NKVD went about its work through an elaborate scenario of political repression. Arrests and widely publicized show trials of local party leaders were followed by carefully planned preparations for the forcible removal of designated insurrectionists. Overseers in these designated areas were NKVD *troikas* ('threesomes'), three individuals who were answerable solely to the Special Council of the NKVD and who were in charge of 'extrajudicial punishment' – a typical obfuscation that meant no prior judicial procedure was needed for deportation, imprisonment or death sentence.

Opposite: Although both Stalin and Beria were Georgian, the Soviet regime oppressed Georgians as severely as other ethnic groups. In 1922, 18 months after Soviet forces had invaded independent Georgia, Beria became first head of the Georgian *Cheka*, then the Georgian GPU. From the mid 1920s, Beria's police carried out purges of nobles and intellectuals, as well as politicians and public servants, scores of whom, as seen here, were put to forced labour and public works schemes.

KOREANS AND UKRAINIANS

On the pretext of countering Japanese espionage, Koreans were targeted, like these individuals, seen in 1933 working in a Siberian labour camp. Within four years, Korean prisoners had spread all over central Asia.

Troikas worked overtime to remove more than 172,000 Koreans from the border regions of Russia's Far East in September and October 1937, an act authorized by the Party's Central Committee and undersigned by Molotov and Stalin. The justification was the need 'to suppress the penetration of Japanese espionage into the Far Eastern Krai ['region']'. In the removal of the Koreans, the role of the NKVD, then headed by Beria's predecessor Yezhov, was supervised by Genrikh Lyushov, a ruthlessly loyal hatchetman from the days of the Chekists. High in government favour, he was transferred from Rostov to become chief of the Far Eastern Krai. The vast steppe of Central Asia, now Kazakhstan, was selected as one of the chief destinations for the Koreans, an unpopulated region with rolling grasslands that had been used for centuries as nomadic grazing grounds.

Another chief area for deportations was the Ukraine, worked for centuries by Polish farmers. For them, living side by side with German minorities, the first waves of deportations came in 1936. How the MVD (*Ministerstvo Unutrennikh Del*, Ministry of Internal Affairs) at the behest of the NKVD went about their work was illustrated by the experiences of those living in the prosperous Ukrainian village of Zytomierz. On one summer night, State Security officials ordered the village council to assemble. Its leaders were informed that families were to be deported to unspecified destinations 'for their own good'. The doors of houses were locked, the men held in custody. Families were ordered to pack their belongings and sell their livestock, preparatory to being stuffed into cattle trucks for the two-week rail journey to Kazakhstan, where the steppe was marked by dry blazing heat in summer and heavy falls of snow and freezing temperatures in winter. On arrival, one family, some of whose members subsequently survived, were marched to a stretch of high grass, featureless save for a newly dug well and a signpost reading 'Village Number 2'. The humiliation was calculated: many of the deportees were literally dumped onto the steppe with no tools, forced to make bricks from mud and straw and learn how to burn animal dung to cook their food. Many did not survive beyond their first winter. Those who did were designated either 'special settlers' or 'enemies of the state' – in effect, they were inhabitants of rural labour camps. All movement was strictly monitored. The observance of religious faith and the Polish language were forbidden under the ever-present threat of arrest by agents of the MVD.

> The humiliation was calculated: many of the deportees were literally dumped onto the steppe with no tools and forced to learn how to burn animal dung to cook their food.

The next wave of Poles to be removed from their homes followed the Russo-German pact, signed on 28 September 1939, confirming the division of Poland between the two states. During the following two years, an estimated 1.5 million Poles, designated 'socially dangerous' or anti-Soviet, were deported to Kazakhstan and to Siberia.

THE BALTIC STATES AND THE VOLGA GERMANS

When it came to the Baltic states occupied by the Soviet Union in the summer of 1940, Ivan Aleksandrovich Serov (1905–63), a Deputy Head of the NKVD and later head of the KGB, issued instructions that were icily specific: 'Operations shall begin at daybreak. Upon entering the home of the person to be deported, the senior member of the operative group shall assemble the entire family of the deportee into one room … In view of the fact that a large number of deportees must be arrested and distributed in special camps and that their families must proceed to special settlements in regions, it is essential that the operations of removal of both the members of the deportee's family and its head shall be carried out simultaneously, without notifying them of the separation confronting them.'

Poles, Latvians, Estonians and Lithuanians were among the victims, their sufferings worsening in 1940 when the Soviet Union occupied the

Deportation by the Soviet security forces of some 15,000 Latvians – among them 2400 small children – took place in mid-June 1941. They were herded into cattle wagons, where they spent weeks, even months. No mention was made in Latvia's Soviet-censored newspapers; thus those left behind were unable to discover what had happened to the deportees.

Baltic states. Conditions on the journeys to exile were appalling. Each truck had a single crude hole cut in the wooden floor to serve as a latrine. The sparse diet of soup, bread and salt fish led inevitably to deaths from dehydration among infants and the elderly. Attempts at escape by ripping open the floors of the trucks could prove fatal: guards fitted a steel scythe beneath the last freight car, ensuring that escapees were cut in half.

Stalin's obsession with the threat of disloyalty among minorities hardened still further with Operation *Barbarossa*, the German assault on the Soviet Union, launched on 22 June 1941. The slightest hint of collaboration or friendship with the invading Germans, many of whom were welcomed as liberators against Communist oppression, led to vast deportations. As to those Germans whose forebears had emigrated to Russia some two centuries before, all were considered to be collectively guilty of spying for the enemy and moves against them were stepped up as the Germans advanced rapidly through the Ukraine towards the Caucasus.

Among the first of the deportees to Kazakhstan and Siberia were the Volga Germans, who in the mid- to late-eighteenth century had founded colonies on unsettled Russian steppes abutting the banks of the Volga river. The fact that many of the succeeding generations no longer had any ties with their country of origin and spoke no German counted for nothing. Also condemning them was their resolute adherence to their Lutheran faith, which had long incurred the hatred of the anti-religious Bolsheviks. On 28 August 1941, Stalin issued a formal Decree of Banishment, along with the abolition of the Volga German Autonomous Soviet Socialist Republic, which dated from the Russian Revolution.

Just how brutal the Volga ethnic cleansing was can be gathered from the experiences of deportees from the district of Obermonjour. Given just four hours to be ready for evacuation, they were herded to the banks of the river, where they boarded barges on the way to the railhead. Each individual, regardless of age, was permitted only one suitcase or bundle before being loaded into freight and cattle cars. Some, anticipating exile to the forests and mines of Siberia, took all the clothes and bedding they could manage, along with pitifully meagre food supplies. The Volga republic had only a single railroad with no branch lines, which necessitated long walks for many to the nearest station. One hundred and fifty-one convoys were embarked from 19 stations. Many of the elderly died, as did those who had attempted to hide in their own homes, only to be dragged out and shot. Among the Volga Germans as a whole, it has been calculated that between 3 September and 21 September 1941 some 366,000 were removed to Siberia.

> 'A single death is a tragedy, a million deaths is a statistic.'
>
> —attributed to Stalin

The Kalmyks, Buddhists and Orthodox Christians from lands lying between Volgograd and the Caspian had, in the words of Professor Donald Rayfield in his book *Stalin and His Hangmen*, 'been for centuries a football kicked between the Russian and Chinese empires'. The charge of handing cattle to the Germans was the pretext for the abolition of this autonomous republic and the creation of a diaspora stretching from the Arctic to eastern Siberia The number of deportees, the majority of whom were put to forced labour, was so vast that no reliable figures exist, although it has been estimated that by 1943 some 93,000 had been dispersed.

THE CRIMEAN TARTARS

The region known today as Chechnya, in the North Caucasus, had been absorbed by Tsarist Russia in 1859. With its Muslim population, it was known as the Checheno-Inguish Republic, and the Chechens waged an endless war for independence. In the 1920s the Soviet Union created autonomous regions for both the Chechen and Inguish, only to place them together again in 1934. This followed the urging of Beria for the NKVD and of officials of the GKO (*Gosudarstvennyy Komitet Oborony* – Soviet State Committee for Defence).

The task of masterminding deportation was entrusted to Efum Evdokinov, a former convict and bibulous crony of Stalin's who had been OGPU chief of the area where overall responsibility resting with Serov. The project was termed a 'general operation', a cloak for what turned out to be one of the

A Wehrmacht soldier carries bread given to him by Ukrainian girls in 1941, the first year of Operation *Barbarossa*. If these Soviet citizens were caught by the NKVD, they would certainly have been deported, along with their families.

most cold-blooded instances of mass deportation. The prisons in Grozny came under the control of the NKVD and of Bogdan Kobulov. A burly Caucasian and one of the most notorious of Beria's lieutenants, he was given to assaulting his victims with fists, then jumping on them before beating their skulls with his stock of blackjacks. The jails were soon bulging with 5000 prisoners, while a further 9000 were placed in hastily commandeered buildings.

The year 1944 also saw the forcible removal of some 160,000 Tartars of the Crimea, who had inhabited the peninsula for more than seven centuries.

They had long experienced repression; occupation by Russian forces in 1783 had led to increasing numbers quitting their homeland for the sprawl of the Ottoman empire, bringing with them a variety of Turkic tongues – a family of languages spoken by numerous nationalities in Russia, Central Asia and Kazakhstan. The Soviet justification for the deportation of the Tartars, along with Greeks, Armenians and Bulgarians, was that they collaborated in large numbers under the German occupation of the peninsula. Responsible once again were Kobulov and Serov, who accused Tartar forces of deserting to the Germans. They also lost no time in informing Beria, who told Stalin of 'the undesirability of Crimean Tartars residing any longer in a frontier zone'.

A deadline for deportation was set for the month of April, the dispersal to be undertaken by the NKVD and NKGB with its own secret police, headed by Vsevolod Merkulov, one of Beria's most trusted colleagues. In fact, the dispersal was completed two weeks ahead of schedule. The homes and farms of the dispersed Crimean Tartars no longer existed. A proud populace of fishermen and vineyard owners had gone, elbowed out to provide villas and sanatoria for Soviet officials.

Living conditions were at their worst in Kazakhstan, where deportees were herded into barracks without windows and were expected to subsist on

DEPORTED TARTARS

Principal destinations for Crimean Tartar deportees included Uzbekistan, Kazakhstan and Tajikistan. Accounts of the journeys of two deportees survived: '... It was a journey of lingering death in cattle trucks, crammed with people, like mobile gas chambers. The journey lasted three to four weeks and took them across the scorching summer steppes of Kazakhstan. They took the Red partisans of the Crimea, the fighters of the Bolshevik underground, and the Soviet and Party activists. Also invalids and old men. The remaining men were fighting at the front, but deportation awaited them at the end of the war. And in the meantime they crammed their women and children into trucks, where they constituted the vast majority. Death mowed down the old, the young and the weak. They died of thirst, suffocation and the stench ... On the long stages, the corpses decomposed in the huddle of the trucks, and at the short halts, where water and food were handed out, the people were not allowed to bury their dead and had to leave them besides the railway trucks'.

Another account reads: 'At 3.00 am (May 18 1944) two soldiers knocked on the door. I was the oldest daughter. I had four younger sisters. The soldiers told us: "You've got 15 minutes and then we are going to take you away". Our father reminded us about the Germans. And how they had gone around collecting the Jews and then shooting them. He was convinced they were going to do the same for all of us. So he told us not to bother taking anything with us – that we were all going to be shot. So we left with only the clothes on our backs. It was only that night that they put the people in our village into trucks and took us to the railroad. When we arrived in Uzbekistan it was 43° Centigrade (110° Fahrenheit) – unimaginable heat. I was the only one to survive. My father, mother and sister all perished from the ordeal.'

Construction of the north and south sections of the Turkestan–Siberia railway was well under way by April 1930. The Gulag system of forced labour survived Stalin's death in 1953 and was still running, although diminishing, in the 1980s.

a bread ration of 150 grams (5 ounces) a day. Two key telegrams, latterly obtained from released KGB archives, were despatched to the leaders ultimately responsible for the mass deportation. On 19 May 1944, Stalin and Molotov were informed: 'The NKVD of USSR reports on the current situation of the Special Operations of Crimean Tartars' Deportation. By the end of May 19, 165,515 persons were brought to different train stations. 136,412 persons were loaded on trains, and sent to their destination of exile. The operation continues. L. Beria, People's Commissar of USSR.'

On 20 May, Kobulov informed Beria: 'We are notifying you that the operation of the Deportation of Crimean Tartars which began on May 18 1944, as you demanded, is concluded today at 16.00 hours. Altogether 173,287 persons were deported by loading them on 67 different trains. Sixty-three trains loaded with people are on their way, the remaining four trains will depart today … Altogether, 191,044 Crimean Tartars were deported.'

However, the deportation of the Tartars was not yet complete, and for Kobulov came a rude awakening. In a mood of tipsy self-congratulation following a lavish bestowal of medals, he threw a banquet. Then, by chance, he learned that a group of Tartars was still at large in a number of villages around Arabat Bay, southwest of the Sea of Azov. Conscious that if news of the lapse reached Beria there could be only one consequence, Kobulov panicked, declaring that 'heads would roll' if within two hours a single Tartar remained alive. A boat was hastily commandeered. The remaining Crimean Tartars, mostly women and children, were forced aboard, then taken to the deepest waters of the Azov Sea, where the boat was hastily scuttled. Those who escaped drowning fell to the machine guns of Kobulov's waiting men.

Those Tartars who survived elsewhere faced high mortality rates due to disease and starvation. Conscious of an earlier typhus outbreak among North Caucasians, the NKVD feared that an epidemic among the deported Crimeans could spread to the general population. On 5 December 1944, Colonel Kuznetsov, Chief of the Section of Special Settlements of the NKVD, wrote to V.V. Chernyshov, a deputy chief of the NKVD, alerting him to a potential typhus epidemic. The warning came too late. Deaths among Crimeans the following year rose to 15,997. By 1 July 1948, the total of deaths in the settlements reached 44,887.

Inevitably, the oppressive methods of the wholesale deportation of the Crimean Tartars attracted only limited attention beyond Asia, sidelined by the war still raging with Germany. Even so, Moscow deemed it necessary to offer some justification to its Allies. Accordingly, Resolution 5859 of the

Clad in German uniforms, Cossack volunteers fighting for the Nazis in 1942 were primarily Crimean Tartars rebelling against the Soviet deportations. Their effectiveness was limited, partly because Hitler was obstructive to any participation by Soviet citizens, largely on racial grounds. However, with the deterioration of Germany's military situation in 1943, he was forced to approve the Cossacks' inclusion.

GPU outlined the official Soviet explanation for the deportations. This was that 'In the period of the Fatherland war many Crimean Tartars betrayed the Motherland, deserted from units of the Red Army defending the Crimea, and turned over the country to the enemy, joined German-formed voluntary Tartar military units to fight against the Red Army in the period of occupation of the Crimea by German-Fascist troops and participated in German punitive detachments.

Crimean Tartars were particularly noted for their brutal reprisals towards Soviet partisans, and also assisted the German occupiers in organizing the

SIBERIAN LABOUR CAMPS

Siberia, the world's most notorious penal colony, gets its name from the Tartar word 'Sibar', meaning 'sleeping land'. A vast region covering virtually all of northern Asia, it extends eastward from the Ural Mountains to the Pacific Ocean and southward from the Arctic Ocean to the hills of north central Kazakhstan and the borders of both Mongolia and China. All but the extreme southwestern area of Siberia lies in Russia, making up about 56 per cent of the country's territory.

Siberia has a history as a place of punishment and exile for political prisoners dating back to the seventeenth century, when Russia annexed Western Siberia. Already at that time, it was being used as a penal colony and a place of exile for political prisoners. However, it first became notorious in 1825, when members of the Decembrist Conspiracy, consisting of radical groups seeking to end serfdom and introduce western reforms under the reign of Tsar Nicholas I, were sent there. Large-scale Russian settlement began in earnest with the construction of the Trans–Siberian Railway, which spurred the development of coal mining. There was also a bid by the interior minister P.A. Stolypin under Nicholas II to reduce rural overpopulation in European Russia and encourage Siberian colonization.

In the closing phases of the Russian Civil War in 1918, an autonomous Siberian government was superseded by the counter-revolutionary Admiral Kolchak, who made his capital at Omsk. White forces were aided by contingents of Tsarist political exiles and the Czech Legion, a group of Austrian army deserters. Most of Siberia was in White hands by late 1918, but the revolution was doomed, following the murder that year of Tsar Nicholas II and his family. Early in 1920, the government fell apart and Kolchak was executed.

Stalin was among many leading revolutionaries who knew the terrain of Siberia well and its effectiveness as a centre for punishment. His first experience there was in the Vologda region, where he was sent into exile after attending a political demonstration. A subsequent arrest led to him being sent to the remote Yenisei-Turukhansk region in northern Siberia, with a population of 12,000 scattered in settlements hundreds of miles apart. It lay north of the Arctic Circle, the temperature in winter fell below -40° Celsius (-40° Fahrenheit), and the Arctic winter nights lasted for eight to nine months. Summer was no more comfortable: it produced plagues of mosquitoes.

Forced Collectivization

Agricultural colonization was achieved by the compulsory resettlement of large segments of the Russian rural population, notably the kulaks. Consequently, the population doubled between 1914 and 1946, with the use of forced labour ubiquitious in the gold mines of East Siberia.

sending to Germany of forced labour and the mass destruction of Soviet people. Crimean Tartars actively collaborated with the German occupying powers, participating in the so-called 'Attar National Committees' organized by German intelligence, and were extensively used by the Germans to infiltrate the rear of the Red Army with spies and diversionists. 'Tartar National Committees', in which the leading role was played by White Guard-Tartar émigrés, with the support of the Crimean Tartars, directed their activity at the persecution and oppression of the non-Tartar population of the Crimea and conducted work 'in preparation for the forcible separation'.

During the period of the First Five Year Plan (1928–33), forced labour was instrumental in mining coal and, above all, building the iron and steel complex of the Kuznetsk Basin, ultimately one of the world's richest coal mining areas.

After the Revolution the labour camps were closed down, only to be reopened by Stalin. The worst of these was probably at Kolyma, in north-eastern Siberia, where temperatures could drop to -90° Celsius (-130°Fahrenheit) during the winter. Around 30 per cent of the prisoners died each year. In 1930, there were 179,000 slaving in the Gulags; five years later the figure reached around a million.

Almost any offence committed against the regime could lead to a sentence in the Gulag. Kulak peasants accused of 'individualistic tendencies' were among the most common inmates, but others included artists who did not conform to 'Socialist Realism'; those with strong religious beliefs, including Catholics, Baptists and members of the Ukrainian Orthodox Church; and people who lived abroad or who had relatives outside Soviet Russia and were in danger of falling under the influence of non-Communists.

Numbers swelled during World War II, those enslaved being 'collaborators', prisoners of war, and men and women taken from Nazi Germany, whether or not they were guilty of anti-Soviet sympathies. Siberia's economic development increased dramatically during the war, with the transfer of many industries from Soviet Europe to the other side of the Urals, where it was intended that they would be less vulnerable to capture by the Germans. Siberian grain proved vital to the Soviet Union's resistance to the German onslaught, despite the loss of valuable agricultural land to the west. Agriculture in Siberia suffered badly during Stalin's collectivization campaign, a policy that was destined to be reversed by Premier Nikita Khrushchev's 'virgin lands' programme. This focused on cultivation in the steppes of southwest Siberia and northwest Kazakhstan.

With the Seven Year Plan (1958–65) came construction of large thermal and hydroelectric powerplants in Siberia and elsewhere. One of the earliest events to highlight the eroding authority of Communism was the opposition to the destruction of natural areas and gross waste of resources, typified by the polluting of Lake Baykal, said to be the world's deepest. Environmental groups banded together to challenge the Communist party's decision.

Since the fall of the USSR Siberia has become more open to foreign travel and trade, but certain of the areas established by Stalin remain unmapped and restricted to foreign visitors. It is thought that these may be within the areas of the previous Siberian forced labour and concentration camp network.

This aerial photograph taken in the 1990s shows the rotting, wooden remnants of a gulag labour camp at Pevek. Located in the Siberian Far East, Pevek is on the edge of the Arctic Circle – a harsh, forbidding place from which escape would have been impossible for most inmates.

The final disposal of the Crimean Tartars was followed by Beria's plans to deport the Bulgarian, Greek and Armenian minorities from the peninsula. The Bulgarians were accused of preparing bread and supplies for the Wehrmacht, assisting the German military in finding and detaining Red Army forces and Soviet partisans, and receiving what were termed 'protective licences' from the German High Command. As for the Greeks, they were alleged to have assisted the Germans with trade and transport. Predictably, Beria recommended to Stalin the wholesale deportation of these communities. Penal settlements established by the NKVD in Uzbekistan received an estimated 3650 Turkish, Greek and Iranian citizens who had been living in the Crimea.

By the closing months of 1944, some 20,000 NKVD troops, together with vast quantities of rolling stock, had been diverted from the war effort for the task. Vast numbers of completely defenceless people – mostly the old, women and children – were removed for resettlement in areas that were totally unequipped to receive them. For example, in just one week in

February 1944, some 500,000 Chechens and Ingush were crammed into 180 train convoys and deported.

It took until three years after Stalin's death for condemnation of the deportations to be voiced within Soviet Russia itself. In February 1956, Nikita Khrushchev declared them to have been 'a violation of Leninist principles'. In a so-called 'Secret Speech' to the 20th Party Congress he declared that the Ukrainians had avoided such a fate 'only because there were too many of them and there was no place to deport them'.

By no means all those who had been displaced by Stalin's deportations were allowed to return to their traditional lands at the war's end. Although decrees were issued for the restoration of, among others, the Chechen-Ingush autonomous Republic, there were exceptions. Most notable among these were Karachays and Balkars – Turkish Caucasians whose territory had been overrun by the Germans in 1942. Despite their resistance to Nazi atrocities, they were branded traitors, and, following the retaking of the area by the Red Army in the following year, were despatched wholesale to Siberia. The denial of resettlement during Khrushchev's rule created tensions and disputes whose effects are felt to this day, most notably in the Caucasus regions.

Some grim relics of Stalinism were still in evidence in the late 1980s. These remnants of a snow-covered barbed wire fence and guard tower were discovered at what had been a Siberian convict camp.

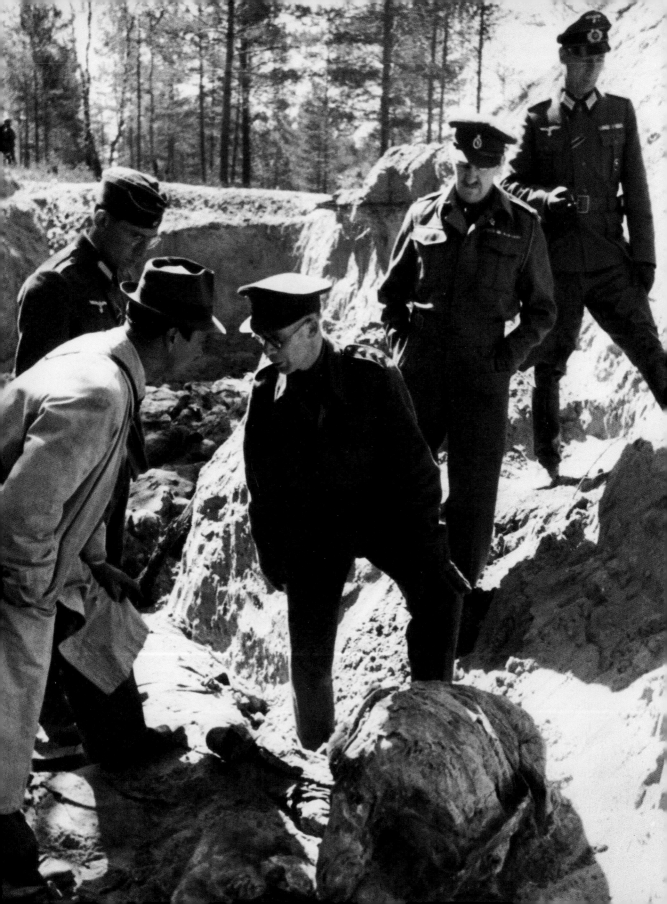

CHAPTER 6

SOVIET TRAITORS

As fortunes turned steadily against Germany, Stalin began preparations for the conquest of Eastern Europe and the post-war establishment of Communism. Stalin saw opposition everywhere, even condemning those captured or wounded in battle as traitors.

B
y the summer of 1943, what is widely regarded as the turning point of the war in Europe had been marked by the German disaster of the Battle of Kursk. This was an attack on a vast and dangerous Russian salient, or bulge, extending from the north of Kharkov to Orel around the industrial city of Kursk itself. More than 6000 tanks clashed. For the first time, the Red Army was able to check a Nazi *blitzkreig*. The advance of the Red Army now seemed unstoppable. Other triumphs included the Soviet offensive in the Ukraine, which began the following Christmas. The Red Army went on to free the region, plunging into Poland across the Dnestr river and into Romania. The Red Army soaked the Crimea in blood, smashing a 122,000-strong Axis force in 35 days, followed speedily by the taking of the fortress city of Sevastopol. Along with the Red Army, which triumphantly gained control, came added muscle for the NKVD.

'TRAITORS, DESERTERS AND COWARDS'
Never before had power tasted so satisfying for Lavrenti Beria. In the areas overrun by the Red Army, he masterminded the creation of Special Departments, activated with the remit to seek out 'traitors, deserters and cowards'. The origins of the Departments – OO, *Osobyi Otdel* – went back to

Opposite: In this photograph taken in 1943, British prisoners-of-war are shown by their German captors the remains of the many thousands of Polish army officers massacred at Katyn, Poland. The Nazi regime hoped that the revelation would provoke dissent among the Allies.

1919, when Lenin and Felix Dzerzhinsky, the head of the *Cheka*, were seeking complete control of the armed forces. Within two months of the Soviet victory at Stalingrad, the Departments had been amalgamated within the NKVD to become SMERSH (*Smert Shpionam* – Death to Spies). Its head was Viktor Abakumov (1908–1954), a womanizer and jazz fanatic, notorious as a specialist in torture and brutality, and later considered to have been a major figure in organizing the murder of more than 4000 Polish officers in the forest of Katyn near Smolensk in the spring of 1943. His position within SMERSH was a mere step on the career ladder. He went on to control the Soviet foreign espionage network that became known as the Information Committee (KI – *Komitet Informatsii*).

Much of the responsibility for the NKVD's overall role, both covert and active, fell to the corpulent Caucasian Bogdan Kobulov and his Belorussian Commissar Lavrenti Tsanava. Penetration was deep within the Red Army, embracing every level of command down to divisional level. Members ranked as officers, wearing the uniform and insignia of the units to which they were attached. This enabled them to conceal their chief function, which was to root out any signs of dissidence, rebellion or 'rumour mongering' both at command level and among front-line troops. Since they were already seasoned practitioners in interrogation, they were able effectively to examine all troops who had managed escape from the Germans. If any of them expected congratulations, they were swiftly disillusioned. At first, being captured merely invited deep suspicion. That hardened in 1941 with the appearance of Order 270, which laid down that all who had surrendered preparatory to being taken prisoner were traitors and, without the recourse to appeal, were promptly shot. They were required to produce witnesses that they had neither deserted or panicked, nor abandoned their weapons and posts. NKVD Special Camps were set up to house suspect escapees.

The wounded were treated with the greatest suspicion, their injuries closely examined to determine whether or not they had been self-inflicted. Deserters – or those who had simply got lost – were shot on the orders of the military tribunal. Those who had been picked up minus their tunics and papers attracted the gravest suspicion, since it was known that commissars, overcome by panic, had got rid of damning

THE KATYN MASSACRE

The bodies of more than 15,000 Polish troops and prominent civilians, murdered in 1940, were discovered in mass graves in the Katyn Forest near the Russian city of Smolensk in the spring of 1943. Their hands were bound and all had been shot in the back of the head. When Nazi occupation forces announced the discovery, Germany hoped that publicity would provoke international revulsion over a Soviet atrocity, thus sewing dissent among the Allies. American and British soldiers, who were German prisoners-of-war, were taken with press representatives to view the massacre site, where a German doctor performed an autopsy on one of the bodies, as seen in the photograph on page 92. The shootings were officially blamed on the Germans until 1992 but, after mounting international pressure, Russian President Boris Yeltsin presented to the Polish President Lech Walesa a copy of the original 1940 execution order signed by Stalin and five other *Politburo* members.

evidence of the stitched star on their sleeves, since Hitler had ordered in March 1941 that all commissars be shot out of hand, saying in the infamous 'Commissar Order' that, 'The Commissars are the bearers of ideologies directly opposed to National Socialism. Therefore the Commissars will be liquidated. German soldiers guilty of breaking international law … will be excused'. The families of those who had surrendered in dubious circumstances were also subject to NKVD terror. Stalin's almost pathological xenophobia extended to condemnation of those who had been stranded in Europe. The mere fact that Soviet citizens had experienced contact with other peoples beyond the frontiers was deemed to have contaminated them. Orders were given to SMERSH that as many of these as possible were to be brought home.

By October 1944, 354,590 former Soviet POWs were screened and some 36,000 arrested, often for inexplicable reasons. In July of the same year, a Soviet pilot, Senior Lieutenant Mikhail Petrovich Deviataev, with a record of nine enemy 'kills', had been shot down and captured by the Germans. He then managed with nine other Soviet POWs to hijack a German bomber and fly it back to Soviet lines. His sole reward was prompt arrest and despatch to a Gulag, where he spent 12 years.

Soviet prisoners captured by the Germans in the Ukraine during 1941. In all, some 5.7 million Soviet army personnel fell into German hands in World War II. An estimated 3.3 million, or about 57 per cent of those captured, were dead by the war's end, victims of Nazi racial policy or murder by German ground forces.

An NKVD officer's pass entitled the holder to almost unlimited powers. During World War II, his duties included ensuring rear area security, restriction of movement and prevention of desertion. The NKVD and later NKGB (responsible for international security) carried out stop-and-search, mass arrests, deportations and executions, including participants in anti-Nazi resistance movements like the Polish *Armia Krajowa*.

THE POLISH PARTISANS

Among the chief victims of the terror squads were Polish partisans, who fondly believed that their task had been to fight Germans. When rounded up, they were either forcibly enrolled in Soviet-controlled units or shot, often on a whim. Punishment battalions were also formed and given what proved to be the most dangerous tasks of all: infiltrating sectors known to be mined or being forced to participate in attacks in the teeth of concentrated German defences. *Armija Krajowa* (the Polish Home Army) in the summer of 1944 launched an uprising in Warsaw against the Germans, hoping for help from the Red Army who were on the opposite bank of the Vistula. Although the Soviets from their positions to south and east could clearly see the burning buildings and palls of smoke, they took no immediate action, letting the Germans destroy the Polish capital block by block.

The British Prime Minister Winston Churchill had pressed the case with Stalin for the right of the government-in-exile to return as Poland's post-war government, pointing out that these Poles were already making a significant contribution, fighting against the Germans in Italy as well as training for the upcoming cross-Channel invasion. But Stalin's intention was to seize total control in eastern Europe and he had long cherished plans to have a pro-Soviet group exercising power in post-war Poland. The Home Army, loyal to

RICHARD SORGE

Early on the morning of Thursday, 23 October 1941, Major General Eugen Ott, German ambassador in Tokyo, sent a telegram to Berlin reporting the arrest of Dr Richard Sorge, special correspondent of the leading newspaper *Frankfurter Zeitung*, and Max Klausen, another German national. Both were detained by the Japanese for 'maintaining treasonable connections' – diplomatic code for charges of espionage.

The news of the detentions spread quickly through Tokyo's German community. An accomplished journalist with high-level contacts in the Japanese government, Sorge was also an agent for German military intelligence, the *Abwehr*. A skilful networker, he drew on the friendship of Major General Ott, whom he had persuaded to give him the job of editing the embassy news bulletin, which meant reading and drawing on official press releases from Berlin.

In fact, much of the information found its way to the espionage headquarters at Moscow Centre. For Sorge, a half-Russian, was a loyal communist, who in the late 1920s had joined the GRU (*Glavnoye Razvedovatel'noye Upravlenie* – Main Intelligence Administration), the military counterpart of the KGB. He was born in 1895 in Adjikent, and moved to Germany with his family when he was three years old. After university, Richard Sorge joined the German Communist Party. Here he was recruited as a junior agent within the Intelligence Division of the Comintern.

Groomed for a role in counter-espionage, he was despatched, under his cover as a journalist, to various European countries with orders to test the strength of Communist feeling. Then he moved to China, where he stuck to his cover editing the output of the German news service. His associates, included Max Klausen, a GRU radio operator and Hozsumi Ozaki, a Communist sympathizer working for another Japanese newspaper.

When it came to Tokyo, his next posting, Sorge was briefed to focus on Japan's plans in the Pacific, and steered in the direction of contacts who would be of special value. Between 1933 and 1934, Sorge fashioned an elaborate intelligence network, aided by Ozaki. Sorge's charm stood him in good stead: even Japan's Prime Minister Fumimaro unknowingly provided information to the spy ring. Such was Sorge's efficiency that his cover remained intact for over six years.

As might have been expected, the SD (SS Intelligence Department) sent their top Gestapo agent to Tokyo to test Sorge's probity. Despite close surveillance, nothing of his true allegiance emerged. Sorge's value to Moscow can scarcely be overestimated, for it was he who warned Stalin about the impending Anti-Comintern Pact in November 1936. He also warned that Germany planned to attack Russia – Operation *Barbarossa*, unleashed on 22 June 1941. However, the warning was ignored. He was also able to report that Japan did not contemplate entering the war against Russia, thus enabling the Russians to shift their Siberian divisions to meet the German onslaught. Sorge's final message to Moscow revealed the impending attack on Pearl Harbor.

Inevitably, the strain of professing loyalty to one country while serving another began to tell. One of his ring broke the rule that new agents were not to be recruited without his sanction. The arrest of one of these made Sorge's own detention inevitable. Ozaki was the first to be arrested, followed by Sorge four days later. Both men were hanged.

Not until 20 years later did the Soviet Union recognize Sorge's services by making him a posthumous Hero of the Soviet Union and putting his picture on a postage stamp.

With Allied forces driving the German Army out of the territories they had occupied, numerous instances of liberation were filmed. Many Soviet newsreels were reenactments for dramatic effect, using the actual participants. Here is a replay of Russian civilians being liberated by their own triumphant forces during 1943.

the London-based government-in exile, stood in his way. Predictably, Ivan Serov, Beria's deputy, condemned it as a criminal band. Some 30,000 arrests were made in Poland by Beria's men. When Soviet troops entered the country, a provisional Polish government, based in Lublin, was set up under Soviet auspices. In response, the soldiers of the Home Army either deserted in droves or threw in their lot with the partisans.

Resistance had to be dealt a decisive blow. Beria set about delivering it with all his serpentine cunning, The new commander of the Home Army, and the successor to its first chief General Bor-Komorowski, was General Leopold Okulicki, who chose to disband his men into autonomous partisan groups. Distrusting the Soviets, Okulicki kept his distance, but in March 1945 he was persuaded by Serov that some form of compromise between the Lublin and London governments could be achieved. Okulicki was then invited in the company of a General Ivanov to fly to London with seven key resistance figures for meetings with Soviet, British and American representatives.

It was an obvious NKVD trap, but Okulicki walked straight into it. No General Ivanov existed. The party was flown not to London but to Moscow, followed by quick transfer to the Lubyanka and prolonged interrogation. A show trial was followed by a prison sentence for Okulicki, which included a period of solitary confinement. His death, attributed to a bowel disorder, was not long in coming; the body was hastily cremated and the ashes dumped in a common grave. The episode was a mere foretaste of the sort of measures Beria was prepared to use.

GENERAL VLASOV

Elsewhere in eastern Europe, Red Army incursions were rapid and decisive. In the east of Czechoslovakia national and red flags were unfurled in every town and village. German refugees, desperately trying to flee to their homes, were left stranded in tightly packed trains abandoned by their drivers; wagons on the roads were immovable, their horses appropriated by the partisans. Industries collapsed, with workers in towns roaming the streets and removing German inscriptions from shop signs.

In the face of mounting revolt in Prague, SS-*Obergruppenführer* Karl Hermann Frank, whom Hitler had appointed Secretary of State in charge of the Reich Protectorate, was facing a Communist opposition that grew more effective by the day. On 9 May, the Red Army entered Prague in the first of two waves, headed by combat troops who indulged in an orgy of raping and looting. Frank was first paralyzed into inaction and then gripped by panic. He ordered the streets to be cleared forthwith, which resulted in surviving sections of the SS to open fire on demonstrators. As the crowds seethed with fury, the Communists pressed their advantage, sending truck loads of supporters to seize the Prague radio station and German administrative offices, By the evening of 5 May, most of these had fallen to the Czechs.

Frank remained sealed within his headquarters at Prague's Hradcany Castle. As for events in the city itself, a single individual had a prime role. To many, General Andrei Andreyevich Vlasov (1900–46) appeared to typify a military tradition that was Prussian, rather than Soviet, an impression strengthened by his austere severity. Yet, paradoxically, Vlasov had been one of Stalin's favoured inner circle. The awards for this peasant's son had been prodigious. In the 1930s, he had received the Order of Lenin and the command of an armoured corps. At the defence of Moscow in 1941, he had distinguished himself still further. Within a year, he had been made Lieutenant General and awarded the Order of the Red Banner. A new command, the Second Shock Army, had taken him

> 'He understood how to win respect, lead men, bind them to himself, and at the same time increase their self-confidence.'
>
> —Soviet newspaper *Red Star* describing General Vlasov, 21 November 1940

The renegade General Andre Vlasov, training with Soviet volunteers in the ill-fated Russian National Army of Liberation, which he hoped could bring about the downfall of Stalin.

to the front during the German assault on Leningrad in March 1942. Bitter fighting centred on the Volkov Marshes, where the Germans benefited from advance intelligence on Russia's deep-seated problems, which included inexperienced personnel, and a lack of heavy artillery and vital air cover. The shock army proved unable to prevent encirclement and, with Stalin refusing to counsel any withdrawal, was annihilated in June. Vlasov, after taking refuge in a peasant hut, was captured the following month.

Although a conscientious and obedient soldier, he had long harboured reservations about the increasing ruthlessness of Stalin's rule, his distaste only increasing with the programme of collectivization and the brutal purges. His dream was to find a way somehow to remove Stalin and Bolshevism, replacing it by a new and truly Socialist regime. Housed in a special camp for prominent prisoners at Vinnitsa in the Ukraine, he wrote to the German authorities, broaching the idea of an anti-Stalin Russian Liberation Army. This, he declared, would attract all Soviet people whose devotion to their country did not extend to Stalin. The propaganda advantages for Germany were eagerly seized by factions within the German High Command, who saw a chance to exploit any splits within the Soviet Union. But the very idea of creating such an army, favoured by Josef Goebbels for its anti-Soviet stance, only served to make Hitler, the obsessive racist, furious. Apart from his rejection of employing a racially inferior Slav, liberation for Soviet Russia was not on the *Führer*'s agenda. His sole intention was to destroy the country root and branch. Orders were given that the collaborators were to be sent to western and southern Europe for front-line duty against the Western Allies.

THE RUSSIAN ARMY OF LIBERATION

For Vlasov this was a disaster. He had not the slightest wish to engage in battle with American or British troops; his sole interest was in freeing Soviet Russia from the grip of Stalin. Only the pressure of events led Hitler to change his mind about the desirability of a liberation army. By September 1944, it had become apparent that everyone available to fight was needed to stem the tide of Soviet vengeance which was approaching from the east. Vlasov's main champion within Germany was Heinrich Himmler, the once-ardent advocate of a German colonial empire in the east. Himmler was now persuaded that the promise of a free Russia could even at this late stage persuade sufficient numbers of Russian soldiers to quit the Soviet ranks.

After touring POW camps in Germany, urging Russians to join the anti-Bolshevik crusade, Vlasov was provided with just two divisions to be concentrated in Prague, considered one of the most vulnerable areas in the face of the Soviet advance. The Russian Army of Liberation was superseded by an impressively sounding 'Committee for the Liberation of the Peoples of Russia' under Chief of Staff Trukin, himself a former Soviet General. A promising beginning allowed for the setting up of an officers' training school, air corps and several units. Two divisions were trained by two other Soviet Generals, Buniachenko and Saitsev. Their men were decked out in German uniforms, but displaying on their shoulder patches and banners a blue St Andrew's cross on a white shield. Their reception was delirious; Prague took swiftly to them as possible liberators from the Soviets.

For Buniachenko, disillusion was not slow in coming. In May 1945, relief at the arrival of a small American patrol assumed to be an advanced contingent of occupying forces was soon replaced by alarm. The US patrol commander explained that his task was to root out any remnants of German resistance – at the same time suggesting that the best plan for Vlasov and his contingent was to await the arrival of the Soviets, reported to be approaching from the northwest. Buniachenko, only too aware of what this would mean, assembled his followers for the great retreat west.

Inevitably, the journey could mean only entanglement amid a chaos of straggling German troops and dispirited refugees, all desperate to reach the American lines before the arrival of the Soviets. Three of Vlasov's generals, travelling apart from the others, were captured by Czech partisans and turned over to the Soviets. The First Division, however, had an easier passage,

General Vlasov is seen conducting an increasingly desperate anti-Soviet recruitment campaign, which produced just two divisions in the defence of Prague. At the end of the war he was disowned by all except the Soviets, who hanged him as a traitor.

This SMERSH officer's card would have been valid until the year 1946. Then the organization, originally formed to arrest 'traitors, deserters, spies and criminal elements', was downgraded to Ministry of Military Forces.

surrendering to the US Third Army. Vlasov's grip on reality grew steadily less sure, and he refused to acknowledge that his status with the Americans was that of a prisoner of war, not an ally. An increasingly irrelevant figure, he continued to pronounce on what he saw as the destiny of Russia shorn of Communism. As for the Soviet commissars, they were content to wait, for a while at least, before pressing anew for the extradition of those they had been instructed to regard as traitors.

THE END OF VLASOV

At 11.00 a.m. on 13 May 1945, Bunichenko was informed by the American commander that the American forces surrounding the First Division would open a path to the east and that the division would be required to march out that afternoon. A number of the troops attempted to hide, while others tried to break out in a bid to get beyond the cordon before the advent of the Soviets. But Allied solidarity remained absolute; US forces closed ranks and drove the men straight into the lines of the Red Army.

Vlasov and his staff, on the other hand, were at the mercy of the US Third Army, which at first proved conciliatory, even sympathetic to their cause. The men were assembled for a suggested parley. On cue, the Soviets appeared and the renegades were overpowered. Vlasov was despatched to SMERSH Front Headquarters near Dresden, and after interrogation was flown to Moscow. A campaign of vengeance now got under way. Wounded followers of Vlasov who had somehow managed to find refuge and treatment in Prague hospitals were dragged from their beds and shot.

Vlasov and his senior colleague, refusing to recant, were subjected to brutal torture before their trials *in camera*, held during January 1946. The death sentences were inevitable. Accounts of the execution vary; one cites the adoption of a method that had been favoured by the People's Courts of the SS. This was to be hanged from piano wire while a hook was dug into the back of the neck.

SMERSH – *Smert Shpionam*

Probably the most sinister acronym in Soviet intelligence, it is believed to have been made up by Stalin himself. Created on 19 April 1943, its remit was to root out elements hostile to Soviet power, particularly in the armed forces. It was headed by Viktor Abakumov, who reported directly to Stalin himself. SMERSH grew out of the Directorate of Special Operations, an integral part of the NKVD, a product of Stalin's obsessive belief that no one in the armed forces, particularly the army, was to be trusted.

SMERSH was divided into five administrative departments. The first was concerned with rooting out perceived defeatism and treachery within every branch of the forces, and no individual from front commander down to the humblest ranker was immune. In addition, those responsible for dissenting political bodies within the services were regarded as prime targets for surveillance. The second was involved in the collation of information and dropping agents behind enemy lines. The distribution and administration of data was the responsibility of the third department, while the fourth was the powerful investigative branch with full powers of arrest. The fifth was divided into three-man tribunals to hear cases and pass sentences. No appeal was allowed, and when executions were ordered these were usually carried out forthwith.

As well as its other functions, SMERSH had a bodyguard role and was well known in the West. Indeed, it had provided the guard for Churchill and Roosevelt during the Tehran Conference, which was held between November and December 1943, and chiefly concerned with the opening of the second front in western Europe.

As World War II came to an end, SMERSH was given the assignment of capturing Adolf Hitler alive. As it turned out, Red Army officers and SMERSH agents found Hitler's partially burned corpse near the *Führerbunker* in Berlin and conducted an investigation to confirm the circumstances of his death. It is thought that the bodies of Hitler and Eva Braun were buried secretly at SMERSH headquarters at Magdeburg until April 1970, at which point they were exhumed and the remains destroyed.

On its disbandment, SMERSH was absorbed into the MGB (Ministry of State Security). This was the forerunner of what became Department V of the First Chief Directorate of the KGB, part of whose function was arranging assassinations of opponents and dissidents.

By 1951, Abakumov's star was waning. He was dismissed and arrested on the orders of Stalin, who considered that he was altogether too close to the power-hungry Lavrenti Beria. Abakumov was also accused of treasonable involvement by party members in Leningrad, a move designed to make the city the capital of an autonomous region within the Soviet Union.

Furthermore, there were well-founded allegations of corruption to answer, not least for appropriating public funds to build luxury additions to his numerous homes. For a time, it seemed that Stalin's death in March 1953 would offer Abakumov his salvation. Beria, preparing his own moves and with an eye on the leadership, ordered Abakumov's release from prison and a return to a security role as his agent. However, Beria himself was arrested that June. One consequence was that Abakumov, in failing health, was back in custody in the Lubyanka, where a team of doctors strove to keep him alive. He was shot in December of the following year.

As to the legacy of SMERSH, its main claim to fame to later generations has been its appropriation by the thriller writer, Ian Fleming, who used it in his series of James Bond novels, most notably the first, *Casino Royale*.

The Russian National Army of Liberation (RONA) was one of the first Soviet volunteer formations created by the Germans, whose members included 15th Cossack Cavalry Corps, seen here in the winter of 1942. They fought against Soviet partisans, and later on the Eastern Front. In the summer of 1944, after heavy losses, RONA was disbanded.

THE FATE OF THE COSSACKS

The forcible repatriation of Soviet citizens who had been prisoners of the Germans continued mercilessly. Little distinction was made between those who had deliberately changed allegiance in exchange for their lives and those who had remained faithful. Prominent objects for vengeance were Cossack generals, whose traditions stretched back to the days of the Tsars and who had thrown in their lot with the Whites in the Civil War following the Russian Revolution.

Many of these had suffered during the collectivization programmes, which had driven them from their highly fertile lands. The mood of jubilation that had been felt by entire populations scenting the end of Soviet domination following the German invasion of 1941 had been caught by sections of anti-Bolshevik forces. These changed sides, pressing into service their highly mobile cavalry squadrons. By 1944, more than 250,000 Cossacks served the Germans, many of whom were recruited into anti-partisan units, reserve

regiments and non-combatant auxiliaries. By the war's end, many were forcibly repatriated.

During the summer of 1945, these included some 50,000 people, including 11,000 women, children and elderly men, among whom were two White generals, 75-year-old Peter Krasnow and Andre Shkuro. All had retreated to a camp in the Austrian village of Gleisdorf, where they were soon tracked down by agents of SMERSH, who requested deportation from the British authorities, anxious to settle the matter quickly. As had been the case with the Polish Home Army commander General Okulicki, plans were laid by the Soviets for an elaborate trap, the responsibility of SMERSH and the NKVD. The Cossack officers were told that a meeting would be arranged with the British commander, Field Marshal Sir Harold Alexander, during the course of which their future would be decided. On 29 May, 1475 of them were loaded into trucks, but their destination was not a meeting with Alexander. Rather, for Krasnow and the other leading Cossacks their fate was 'special treatment' in the cellars of the Lubyanka, which meant maximum humiliation and prolonged torture, ending in death on the gallows.

Russian Cossacks like these in German uniform were widely admired by senior officers in the Wehrmacht. A Cossack cavalry formation in Mohylev, Belorussia, was commanded in 1942 by a former Soviet major, Kononov, who had crossed over with his men. He began his service on the side of the Germans by guarding the line of communications against Soviet partisans.

The infamous Lubyanka prison during the 1970s, the statue of Felix Dzerzhinsky prominent in the foreground. Although the Soviet secret police changed its name many times, its headquarters remained in the building throughout.

SOVIET OCCUPATION

As the Red Army pressed west, the Germans, in desperation, scattered leaflets from the air, encouraging the Soviet troops to believe that changing sides would save their lives. The NKVD combed bombed-out towns for truant soldiers masquerading as civilians. In Berlin, bombed day and night by the Americans and the British, up to three million cubic feet of debris carpeted the streets. Every third house had been destroyed or rendered uninhabitable. Over a million people were homeless, huddling in cellars and air raid shelters. General Reymann, the city commandant, estimated that he would need 200,000 fully trained and equipped troops to defend Berlin's 321 square miles. In fact, he had at his disposal only 60,000 *Volkssturm* (Home Guard) and a motley collection of Hitler Youth. The truth was that no one had the heart to fight any longer. Refugees straggling in from the east gave gruesome accounts of the vengeful atrocities committed by the Soviets; suicide rates were high, thanks to a plentiful supply of cyanide capsules.

By way of contrast, Communists either trapped or imprisoned in Berlin were living for the moment when their liberators would arrive. At considerable risk to themselves and their families, the more militant had over the months organized cells whose members were entrusted with compiling detailed dossiers of every known SS and Gestapo official. These were to be handed to the Soviets on arrival for appropriate action. In the case of one cell in the Neuenhagen-Hoppegarten sector, 19km (12 miles) east of Berlin, plans had also been presented by ardent Marxists outlining their plans for the future administration of the area. Their reception dashed all hopes. Those lucky enough escaped with a mere 'Nyet'. Others faced deportations and the gulags, the latest victims of Stalin's obsessive distrust.

LUBYANKA PRISON

The Lubyanka prison in Moscow was very far from being a jail in the conventional sense. Here, literally thousands, real or imagined opponents of the Soviet regime, were not only confined to cells but subjected to prolonged interrogation and hideous torture. Although executions were carried out behind its walls, many victims were killed elsewhere or shipped to camps within the Gulag.

It was actually a complex of three buildings, and it was the main yellow one that contained the prison and which predates the Russian Revolution of 1917. This was taken over by the Bolsheviks in 1918 as the headquarters of the 'Extraordinary Commission for the Struggle against Counter Revolution, Espionage and Sabotage'. The original Extraordinary Commission, which became the *Cheka*, was first established on Lenin's orders in 1917 by Felix Dzerzhinsky whose staff, in his own words, consisted of 'solid, hard men without pity, who are ready to sacrifice everything for the sake of the revolution'. His directive was: 'Just round up all the most resolute people you can who understand that there is nothing more effective than a bullet in the head to shut people up.'

Today, the old Lubyanka houses the headquarters of the Border Troops and also contains the Directorate of the *Federalnaya Sluzhba Bezopasnosti Rossiyskoy Federatsii,* Federal Security Services of the Russian Federation (FSB), which extends to another of the buildings on the left side.

Before the collapse of the Soviet Union, the open Lubyanka Square was dominated by a 14-ton statue of Felix Dzerzhinsky, but in August 1991 angry crowds, aided by five cranes, tore it down and had it dumped in a park. However, it was argued that it should be restored to the square as an important historical artifact, as well as being, in the words of Moscow's mayor Yuri Luzhow, a 'beautiful architectural and artistic composition'. Instead, by way of compromise, a new statue of Dzerzhinsky was erected a few blocks away at the Interior Ministry.

These days, without fear of arrest, residents and visitors to Moscow can learn something of the grim history of the Lubyanka, at the KGB Museum of Security Service nearby.

They might also get to hear what is probably the Lubyanka's only joke – the one about the prisoner who was invited to peer out of a window on the top floor because on a clear day it afforded an excellent view of Siberia.

REPRESSION

Although repression of enemies, real or imagined, was bad enough in Berlin, they were infinitely worse in East Prussia. On 5 May 1945, three days ahead of the signing of the instrument of surrender at Marshal Zhukov's headquarters in Berlin and five days after Hitler's suicide, Beria sent a memo to Stalin. In it, he stated that he had despatched Colonel General Apollonov with nine NKVD regiments and 400 SMERSH operatives 'to secure the elimination of spies, saboteurs and other enemy elements, and establish the necessary order in the town and ports of East Prussia. For your information, during the Red Army's advance on the territory of East Prussia, NKVD representatives removed from January until April this year over 50,000 enemy elements.' The vague term 'enemy elements' proved especially convenient: it was interpreted in any way that the NKVD thought fit. Stalin's vengeance surpassed all his previous brutalities in Germany. As the result of deliberate planning, land was laid waste, while farmers were forced to abandon livestock, which was either slaughtered or removed to the Soviet Union; low-lying terrain was reduced to swamp. And for trapped civilians came deportation, particularly of women and girls, who were forced into working up to 16 hours a day in inhospitable regions.

Red Army infantry sitting on an SU-100 assault gun move into Soviet-occupied Berlin, May 1945. Frontline troops were inevitably followed by NKVD security forces.

Buildings in Berlin's elegant Elizabetstrasse burn following the final street battles in Berlin, April 1945. The street had been dug up by the German defenders to create rudimentary antitank obstacles. Like Berlin, many cities in eastern and central Europe needed almost totally rebuilding after the war.

After the immolation of East Prussia, terror, already rife in Poland, was intensified with the posting there of 15 NKVD regiments. What this was to mean in terms of future repression was set out in an order from Beria that Comrade Selivanovsky was 'to combine the duties of representing the NKVD of the USSR and councillor at the Polish Ministry of Public Security'. As the war drew to a close, the future of Europe figured increasingly in Allied discussions.

In November and December 1943, Poland's post-war frontiers had been mapped out in preliminary detail when the 'Big Three' Allied leaders had met in Tehran. Inflexible in his role of hard man, Stalin dominated the proceedings, making his wishes clear. What he wanted was a slice of eastern Poland up to 300km (185 miles) wide. By way of compensation, Poland was to gain a slice in the west, cut from the eastern boundary of Germany, extending Poland to the Oder and Neisse rivers.

Another meeting of the trio was held in Moscow in October 1944, prefaced by an elaborate ceremonial greeting for Churchill. Plans were made for the future of the post-war Balkan states, which were further discussed at meetings held at Potsdam and Yalta. Unfortunately, President Roosevelt died on 12 April 1945; his successor Harry Truman was inexperienced in international affairs. Furthermore, a general election in Britain then ousted Churchill, who was replaced by Clement Attlee.

The survivor, Stalin, seasoned, crafty and as ruthless as ever, was at the height of his power at home, free of the restraints of democracy. Moscow controlled East Germany and Poland, the latter a docile buffer between the Soviet Union and potential attackers from the west. A Cold War, destined to last for two generations, was now underway.

CHAPTER 7

IRON EMPIRE

The joy of victory for all Russians at the end of World War II was soon followed by harsh economic realities, the resumption of internal repression and the extension of Soviet power in Eastern Europe.

O n 24 June 1945, Soviet troops paraded in triumph across the rain-splashed length of Moscow's Red Square. From atop the Lenin Mausoleum, Josef Stalin reviewed his victory parade. The other hero of the day was the ruthless peasant Marshal Georgi Zhukov (1896–1974). Nicknamed *Zhuk* (beetle), he had been snatched from a besieged Leningrad to halt the Germans at the gates of Moscow and had achieved even greater successes during the battle of Stalingrad, finally leading the capture of Berlin. Here too was Marshal Konstantin Rokossovsky, another hero of Stalingrad and incidentally a lucky survivor from the days of the purges, who had once been sent to the Gulag on the charge of having 'connections with foreign intelligence'.

The parade was brilliant theatre. Banners and standards carried that day were not those of the Red Army but of Hitler's vanquished *Wehrmacht*. On reaching the mausoleum, the troops threw their trophies at Stalin's feet. The next day, Stalin himself received the tribute of Moscow for the defence of the city four years before. Acclaimed as 'Hero of the Soviet Union', he received the title of *Generalissimo*.

In the feverish climate of victory, the ruthless pre-war measures of collectivization and industrialization, which had allowed Russia to survive were, if not forgotten, at least justified, even at the price of 20 million dead.

Opposite: A day of triumph with the elaborately staged World War II victory parade in Moscow's Red Square. Marshals Zhukov (right) and Rokossovsky led the parade on horseback. Millions thronged Moscow's central districts, the celebrations culminating in a gigantic evening firework display. In a broadcast, Stalin proclaimed that the 'great banner of freedom' could at last be raised.

Hope persisted way beyond the Soviet Union. An article in the *New York Times* declared: 'The Russian system, though greatly different from our own, rests on an expressed ideal of the welfare of the common man. Nor need we doubt in the least that Marshal Stalin and his associates honestly plan, once they have made their frontiers secure … to build up living standards in Russia in an atmosphere of international peace.'

> Stalin's fear of possible postwar rebellions led to exemplary power being granted to the new MGB.

But this optimism was woefully misplaced. After the euphoria came sharp reality: the Soviet Union faced widespread homelessness and starvation, devastated towns and cities and a crippled industrial infrastructure. Along with the recognition of all this came new hope: that reconstruction was already underway, that lives and standards would improve. Stalin, though, perceived a new danger; people in search of something better might well have recourse to rebellion. At all costs there had to be a drive to ensure and maximize control from the centre.

THE MGB

As Deputy Chairman of the Council of Ministers, and not least because of his favoured status with Stalin, Lavrenti Beria continued to co-ordinate the activities of the security apparatus at the highest level. The NKVD was upgraded to ministerial status, while the NKGB, which had co-operated with the former in the wartime deportations, was now rebranded as the MGB (*Ministerstvo Gosudarstvennoi Bezopastnosti*, Soviet Ministry of State Security). Exemplary power was given to one of its sections, the Espionage and Anti-Espionage Department, with the emphasis on military, naval and political espionage.

This department, along with others, became involved with the steady escalation of what became known as the Cold War, with its accompanying tension between East and West. It was an apparatus that was also empowered to stem continued unrest throughout the Soviet empire, particularly among nationalist sympathizers in the Baltic republics, Belorussia and the Ukraine. These were harbouring cadres of anti-Soviet partisans. Isolated areas of rebellion could be dealt with by force of arms, but subtler methods were needed when it came to subduing activists protected by underground groups. Agents, largely volunteers within the MGB, were sent undercover to penetrate the regions, undertaking intensive training courses, becoming proficient in the languages and dialects of the areas where they were to operate and versed in their culture and religious history.

The writer Boris Levytsky, many of whose family had fallen victim to Stalin's purges, left an account of what was required of agents when it came to infiltration: 'Out of these volunteers partisan groups were formed … and sent into the forests. They lived a hard life for months – sometimes, for example in the Carpathians, for years – in the same conditions as their opponents. Their object was to win the confidence of the real partisans. In order to prove their genuiness and trustworthiness they sometimes fought side by side with the real partisans against the Soviets. Only when they knew the whole organization of a partisan unit and all their helpers did they show their true colours and destroy them with the aid of the MGB apparatus.'

The extent of the opposition Stalin faced could be gauged by the fact that partisan groups in Estonia, Latvia, Belorussia and the Ukraine held out in some cases as late as 1952. Highlighting the frequently fragile life of agents and showing how ruthless their controllers were, Boris Levytsky cited the fate of 21-year-old M.Y. Dovsky, cover name 'Zoroka', who, posing as a partisan, operated in the small Ukrainian-Galician town of Rogatyn. Attracting suspicion, he was ordered to prove his probity by murdering Captain Anosov, the Rogatyn MGB chief. Dovsky swiftly contacted his MGB controller who, determined that Dovsky's cover would not be blown, swiftly sanctioned the killing. Still unconvinced, the partisans subjected Dovsky to further heavy grilling, under which he eventually confessed his true allegiance; he, in turn, was shot.

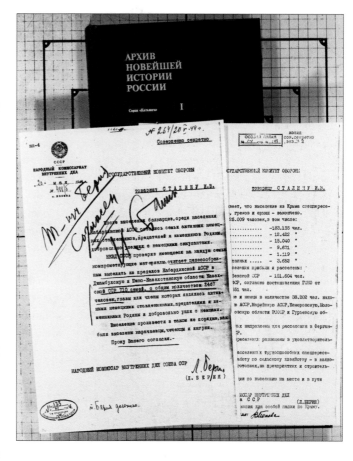

This top secret memorandum was found in Stalin's 'Special Folder' after his death and released to the public in the 1990s. Signed by Beria and approved by Stalin in 1944, the document confirms the forced deportation from the Caucasus to Kazakhstan of some 710 families accused of collaboration with Nazis.

THE GULAGS CONTINUE

The Soviet concentration camps and the Gulags had remained in use throughout the war and many of those who had hoped for amnesty following the defeat of Germany were sorely disappointed. These camps also took on a new role as centres of revenge and punishment for so-called 'collaborators', a term applied to anyone whose loyalty to the Soviet Union was in question. A significant number of these 'collaborators' were women who were accused of having slept with Germans and who were branded as '*s pod nyemtsa*' – having been 'under a German'. Life was particularly harsh for those accused of the most serious political crimes, predominantly espionage. Here

DMITRI SHOSTAKOVICH

There was scarcely any artist of stature who did not feel the burden of censorship backed by political terror. Those who flourished despite repression had to spend their entire careers negotiating the ambiguous and sometimes deadly terrain of Soviet cultural politics. An outstanding example was the St Petersburg-born composer Dmitri Dmitrievich Shostakovich (1906–75), whose most famous works were cycles of symphonies and string quartets as well as operas, six concertos and ballet and film music. To continue working at all, he had to ride an emotional rollercoaster, one moment earning favour – he received two Stalin prizes – and the next working in the teeth of unsparing criticism and abuse, labelled 'cosmopolitan', 'formalist' and anti-Soviet'.

The first of a number of denunciations followed the premiere of Shostakovich's opera *'Lady Macbeth of Mtsensk'*, which initially had been officially praised as written by 'a Soviet composer brought up in the best tradition of Soviet culture'. Zhdanov however thought otherwise and his campaign of petty bullying was typified via an unsigned review in the party newspaper *Pravda*. It stated that the work was cacophonous, perverted, 'alienated appreciative audiences', contained 'deliberate dissonance' and above all was 'musical noise'. After the opera was taken off, a campaign to discredit the composer further was launched. Among the most insulting criticisms was that Shostakovich wrote pieces that no one was able to whistle. In a further insult, Zhdanov, at a meeting with Shostakovich, tinkled on a piano what he held to be acceptable 'people's tunes'.

The persecution, beginning at the time of the Great Terror in which many of the composer's friends and relatives were imprisoned or killed, continued up to Zhdanov's death. A second condemnation in 1948 of Shostakovich for 'formalism' had a more serious outcome. He was obliged to publicly recant, most of his works were banned and his family, subject to constant surveillance, had privileges withdrawn. The theatre producer Yuri Lyubimov revealed that Shostakovich was reduced to fear and 'waited for his arrest at night out on the landing …so that at least his family wouldn't be disturbed'.

In the next few years, because of the ban on his work and the necessity to pay the rent, Shostakovich's compositions consisted of film music and formulaic works aimed at securing official rehabilitation. More serious compositions, for a time at least, went no further than his desk drawer. To continue working, Shostakovich was obliged to recant for a number of past misdemeanours.

Thanks to his previous reputation outside the Soviet Union, which made him a useful ambassador for Stalin, restrictions on his music and living arrangements were eased. But the price was recantation. He wrote 'Song of Forests', a cantata praising Stalin as 'the great gardener' and in 1951 Shostakovich was made a deputy to the Supreme Soviet. Finally, in 1960, he joined the Communist Party, a move which, according to a friend, Lev Lebedinsky, led him to consider the option of suicide. Until his death from lung cancer in 1975, his work became progressively darker and more introspective.

conditions rivalled the very worst of the early Gulags. Neither correspondence nor visits were permitted. Prisoners who were told that they had served their sentences and were therefore being released were treated with especial cruelty. 'Release' meant nothing beyond a stamped piece of paper. Inmates never saw their homes again and furthermore were

required to settle in the vicinity of the camp, continuing the regime of hard labour which had been their original sentence.

'ZHDANOVISM'

There was scarcely a single activity within the Soviet Union, political or professional, which was free from the effects of Stalin's suspicion and desire for revenge. Seemingly tireless in his paranoia, Stalin switched his attention to artists and intellectuals throughout his empire who refused to be constrained by doctrinal straitjackets. The task of initiating a cultural purge was entrusted to Andrei Zhdanov (1896–1948), a gross and gruff heavy drinker who had become party leader in Leningrad after the assassination of Kirov in 1934. According to Molotov, Zhdanov was held in exceptionally 'high esteem by Stalin' – a dubious and dangerous honour, although he enjoyed a measure of protection because his son Yuri had married Stalin's daughter, Svetlana Alliluyeva.

Stalin had a special role for him: the development of a strict ideological code, later known as Zhdanovism, which insisted on strong socialist realism in art, condemning composers, painters, poets and film directors labelled 'bourgeois' and 'reactionary'. The establishment in 1934 of the Union of Soviet Writers was, Zhdanov declared, dedicated to bringing about

Dmitri Shostakovich displays the International Peace Award presented to him at the House of Trade Unions in Moscow on 6 October 1954. Eight days later, his 10th Symphony in E Minor, Opus 93 – thought by many to be his finest composition – was premiered at the Carnegie Hall in New York City.

115

After his death, many within the ranks of the intelligentsia declared that their greatest nightmare was to receive an unscheduled visit from Andrey Zhdanov (left) and be accused of offending against 'the canon of socialist realism'. A bullying drunk, he and his staff attacked writers and editors who failed to praise Stalin sufficiently.

'ideological refashioning' for 'the education of labouring people in the spirit of socialism'. As time went on his power increased. Painters were likely to be granted commissions only if their work celebrated and endorsed the economic and social achievements of the Soviet state. Visitors to galleries were accompanied by official guides and were issued with exhibition notes compiled at the behest of the All-Union Arts Committee, a scrutinizing body set up personally by Stalin. Writers along with composers took the brunt of Zhdanovism. 'Ideologically impure' work was banned from both new and second-hand bookshops and libraries. At the behest of the NKVD, relatives and friends, often subject to threats and blackmail for their own activities, were encouraged to inform on those secretly engaged in forbidden work.

ROMANIA

Also at this time, Stalin was pondering the prospect of an empire lying beyond Soviet Russia. He had long nursed ideas about the future shape of the countries of occupied Eastern Europe, following the defeat of Nazi Germany. Those who were instrumental in installing a Soviet regime in each of the conquered territories became responsible ultimately to Beria.

Romania had been the first of the Nazi satellites to fall, following public discontent with the policy of the dictator General Ion Antonescu. This had led in June 1944 to the creation of a 'National Democratic Block' to bring the country out of the war. Within it, the Communist Party and Social Democrats joined with two small left-wing parties to form the National Democratic Front (FND). On 23 August, the young King Michael announced on the radio that Romania had accepted an armistice offered by the Soviet Union, Great Britain and the United States. Simultaneously, in a dramatic coup, he ordered Antonescu's arrest and announced he would accept Allied armistice terms. Romania declared war on Germany, with the Romanian Army fighting alongside the Soviets. Hitler's riposte was to order the King's arrest, and the reinstatement of Antonescu or a pro-German equivalent. He sent 6000 troops to support existing German forces, but these were soon repulsed.

Antonescu's overthrow was followed by a brief period of euphoria. Preparations for King Michael's *coup d'état*, helped in part by negotiations with the Allies in Cairo, had resulted in the Soviet Foreign Minister Molotov proclaiming: 'The Soviet government declares that it does not pursue the aim of acquiring any part of Romanian territory other than Bessarabia, or of altering the social structure of Romania as it exists at present'. Furthermore, during the meeting of the Allies at Yalta in early 1945 the Soviet Union, Britain and the United States affirmed their commitment 'to build world order under the law dedicated to peace security and freedom'. The promise was also made to help 'the peoples of the former Axis satellite states to solve by democratic means their pressing and political and economic problems'. The Yalta Declaration also declared support for 'free and unfettered elections of the governments responsive to the will of the people'.

> A campaign of intimidation and violence was launched in Bucharest, threatening those who did not support the Communists in the rigged election. Predictably, the Communists secured an 80 per cent majority.

The Soviet Union lost no time in pressing the advantage of its alliance with the FND. The fiery Vyshinsky, summoned from Moscow on 27 February, demanded in an interview with King Michael that he appoint a member of the FND to form a government. The King later related that when Vyshinsky left the room, he slammed the door so hard that he cracked the plaster round it. The post of head of government went to a co-founder of the FND, the Transylvanian Petru Groza, founder of a radical peasant-based organization, the Ploughman's Front.

'FREE' ELECTION

Communists came to dominate the party. Under pressure from Britain and the US, Groza had agreed to hold elections, the idea being to give people a chance to choose their representatives. With a show of belligerence, Groza, in a speech to petroleum workers, declared: 'We shall be victorious in the

Romanian Communist Anna Pauker addresses a pre-election meeting of the Women's Democratic Federation in Bucharest on 17 November 1946. In the new government, she was named foreign minister, earning a cover portrait in the US magazine *Time* with the caption: 'The most powerful woman in the world'. Notoriously outspoken, she condemned Stalin's plans for purging past Romanian Communist leaders. Other targets for her criticism were Soviet-inspired monetary reform and the enforced state collectivization of the peasantry.

election. If the reactionaries succeed, do you think we shall let it live 24 hours? We shall immediately take revenge'. Another leading figure, Gheorghe Tatarescu, said, 'We shall put some in prison, liquidate others and the rest we shall deport'.

In the months leading up to the elections, members of the opposition parties were targeted, and many of them were arrested. Communist hatchetmen stormed meetings, harassing officials and speakers. Known opponents to the FND encountered a wall of bureaucracy when it came to registering their right to vote and securing voting slips. In a censorship clampdown, radio and newspaper campaigning was brought to a halt. Even before polling stations opened, government supporters voted several times, putting their votes in ballot boxes already filled with Government voting slips. Proceedings veered on sheer farce when, after the count, telephone connections to the provinces were cut: many districts had voted predominantly in favour of the opposition parties so that time was needed to falsify the results. Inevitably, it was announced that the FND had won an 80 per cent majority.

However, the United States, at a meeting of foreign ministers in Moscow, denounced Romania's regime as authoritarian and non-representative, calling for Groza to name legitimate members of the opposition parties to cabinet posts. Stalin agreed verbally to make concessions but significantly issued no guarantees. Groza consented to appoint two members of the former parties, National Peasant and National Liberal, but gave them no portfolios. FND ministers dominated the Cabinet.

ABDICATION

The opening by King Michael of a National Assembly shorn of any opposition members was followed by an ominous calm, ending when Moscow without warning instituted a new policy for the Romanian Communists. This bore all the signs of vintage Stalinism. Arrests, which hitherto had been confined to past members of the opposition, were now extended to rank-and-file peasants and workers. Protests at the denial of human rights in Romania were made by Britain and the United States. The Soviet response was to seize leaders of the National Peasant Party, previously the most powerful in the National Democratic Block, and place them under house arrest. Later they were sentenced to penal servitude. Further wrath was turned on the King, who was asked to dismiss members of his household; bravely, he stood his ground and refused.

> 'Anna Pauker…I have always felt when I was with her that she was like a boa constrictor which has just been fed, and therefore is not going to eat you – at the moment!'
>
> —From *I Live Again* by Princess Ileana of Romania

The next move came when King Michael, who had recently become engaged to Princess Anne of Bourbon-Parma, received a request for interview from Petru Groza and Gheorghe Gheorghiu-Dej, the Communist Party Secretary General and a hardline Stalinist. What happened next was told by Michael to the writer Simon Sebag Montefiore:

'They said they wished to see me about "a family matter". So I thought it was about my fiancée …They produced a bit of paper. It was the abdication … The grammar was not good. They could hardly even write; so I would not sign. But they said: "Your guards have been arrested; the telephone has been cut; and there is artillery pointing at this very office". I looked out of the window. Everything they said was true; there was a howitzer pointing at me. I tried to delay, suggesting that we ask the people. "No time to ask the people," they said. "There'll be disturbances and we'll shoot the whole lot and it would be your fault." I was disgusted at how low these people were. And I signed.'

It was also made clear that, had he not signed, he would have been arrested for allegedly plotting with Great Britain and the United States against his own government. Outside, troops of the Soviet-raised Romanian division were in control; tanks surrounded the Elisabeta Palace and the surrounding streets. Michael's dubious consolation for exile was the later bestowal of the American Legion of Merit for making, in the words of President Harry Truman, 'an outstanding contribution to the cause of freedom and democracy'.

Stalin's iron hand now struck against Petru Groza. Power shifted increasingly to Gheorghiu-Dej, an arch intriguer who set out to profit from the mounting anti-Semitism in Soviet policy. Attention focussed on the foreign minister Anna Pauker, an outspoken, fiery Orthodox Jewess, who was described as 'heavy and sluggish with all that is repellent and yet horribly fascinating in a snake'. As a termagant, she attracted Stalin's wrath and the charge of 'cosmopolitanism', a familiar label used against Jews in the Soviet Union and the Eastern Bloc. Fed further criticism, Stalin believed that Pauker was 'too soft'. He told Gheorghiu-Dej, now leading Romania: 'Anna is a good reliable comrade but, you see, she is a Jewess of bourgeois origin, and the party in Romania needs a leader from the ranks of the working-class, a true born Romanian …' Pauker was arrested in February 1952, and subjected to prolonged interrogations, in the course of which she gave considerably more than she got, not hesitating to criticise some of Stalin's policies. Following Stalin's death the following year, her lengthy jail sentence was remitted. All this followed the adoption of a new Soviet-model constitution, which included the reform of local government into a system of Soviets and the compulsory introduction of the Russian language into all schools and universities; Romania became a subservient satellite of the Soviet Union.

BULGARIA

Bulgaria, too, was destined to follow the same route, with Hitler demanding of King Boris III, the country's monarch, that the country, a junior member of the Axis, should join the war against the Soviet Union. The King was shouted down for insisting that Bulgarian neutrality was in everyone's interest, including Germany's. Subsequently, Boris died in August 1943, somewhat mysteriously; it was rumoured that he had been poisoned by Hitler to remove a tiresome obstacle. A regency council took power, announcing Bulgaria's withdrawal from the war on 2 August 1944. Stalin refused to accept, invading Bulgaria the next month, meeting no resistance and compelling Bulgaria to declare war on Germany. An umbrella organization, the Fatherland Front, which consisted of an assortment of Communists,

King Boris III of Bulgaria and Adolf Hitler in August 1936. Five years later, the King was dead, rumoured to have been murdered. His death came after an acrimonious meeting with the Fûhrer. One theory suggests that Boris, who was a bad air traveller, took what he thought was his usual drug to help him on his journey home in a German aircraft, but that another drug had been substituted. Hitler is also said to have ordered the plane to fly unusually high, causing the King to suffer a fatal heart attack after landing.

Agrarians, Social Democrats and the Zveno (Republicans), formed a government. This was dominated by the Communists, who insisted on their own nominees as Minister of the Interior and the Justice Minister.

One of its very first acts was to purge all those held responsible for pro-German policy in Bulgaria since 1941. People's Courts worked tirelessly until March 1945, by which time over 2000 people had been sentenced to death and at least 11,000 to imprisonment. Upwards of 40,000 were shot without trial. The Communists, conscious that they were the smaller party, did everything they could to outsmart their popular rivals, the Agrarians. Their leaders were first attacked by propaganda and arrested, along with many others. Georgi Dimitrov, a popular figure who had returned from exile, was seen off by jealous factions from both Russia and Bulgaria.

Another object of suspicion was Nikola Petrov, an Agrarian and the last significant opposition leader. He was executed in Sofia's Central Prison, allegedly by garrotte.

At this point, Stalin intervened, keen to dispose of a number of personal enemies, including Traicho Kostov, the Deputy Prime Minister. A trusted agent, Lev Shvartsman, was despatched from Moscow with a team of interrogators, whose reports on Kostov were sent for Stalin's perusal. An indictment was drawn up; Kostov was hanged in December 1949, and scores of others went to prison. The Social Democrats, refusing to be intimidated, continued to oppose many of the measures of the Fatherland Front. But their time was running out; by the end of 1949, they had merged with the Communists.

HUNGARY

In Hungary, there was virtually no resistance movement against the Germans during the war and Moscow-trained Communists followed in the wake of the Red Army to seize power. From 1942, Hungary's regent, Admiral Horthy, had cautiously been trying to lessen the country's involvement in the war on the Axis side, and in October 1944 he proclaimed its withdrawal. Following Hungary's withdrawal from the war Hitler launched a failed attempt to rescue the German garrison in Budapest with an SS corps and Panzer army. However, on 13 February 1945, the capital fell to the Red Army, who not

Soviet troops reached Hungary by early 1945. The call went out: 'Turn your arms against the German oppressors and help the Red Army… for the good of a Free and Democratic Hungary.' But, along with the other countries of Eastern Europe, Hungary became an integral part of the Soviet bloc.

long after instituted a reign of terror. A month earlier while Budapest was still under siege, the headquarters of the newly formed Political Police was established by Gabor Peter. A Hungarian who had worked as a Soviet agent with the Red Army during the war, he claimed that the Political Police had the prime task of uncovering and prosecuting Hungarian Nazis. In practice, its mission was more wide-ranging. Peter discovered that, while it was no longer possible for captured Jews to be shipped to Germany, Nazis were still rounding them up on the quays of the Danube, where they were shot and their bodies thrown in the water.

Responsibility for all this rested with Janos Kessmenn, a Hungarian Nazi, considered by Peter to be an ideal target for blackmail as well as a useful source of funds for the Political Police. Kessmenn was arrested and informed that he would escape prosecution if he revealed the whereabouts of a hidden cache of property which had been appropriated from the Jews. He went on to produce $90,000 in foreign exchange, some 1500 carats of diamonds and more than 10,000 assorted gold items. Other useful sources of income included robbery, theft and extortion, most from small shopkeepers. Peter, who knew what was good for him, hastened to maintain close relations with the agents of NKVD, who soon made it clear that those arrested belonged to them. The next step was for the Political Police to be reorganized and established as the AVO (*Allamvedelmi Osztaly*, State Security Authority), headed nominally by Gabor Peter, but swallowed inevitably by the Soviet secret operations apparatus.

> '…Look around in East Europe and see if you can find a country where the Ministry of the Interior is not in the hands of the Communist Party'.
>
> —Matyas Rakosi,
> Hungarian Communist politician

The AVO took on the dimensions of a private army, responsible solely to the Communist Party and possessing virtually limitless powers. No sooner had the country been wholly cleared of the Germans than a Provisional Government took charge, wholly subservient to Moscow. At the elections, the Smallholders Party took 57 per cent of the vote and looked set to form a government, a move spurned by Marshal Kliment Voroshilov (1881–1969), who had commanded Soviet northwest armies in World War II. As Chairman of the Allied Control Commission, he had frequently ignored the British and US members, and he now established a coalition in which the Communists held the key posts. Purges and show trials followed.

ARRESTS AND TRIALS

For a time, considerable authority rested in the hands of Laszlo Rajik, who was not only Minister of the Interior but also in control of the AVO. Making enemies was inevitable. Prominent among them was the Minister of the Interior Janus Kadar, who had been an apt disciple of Moscow's vituperative interrogators. Along with 18 others, Rajik was arrested, accused of being a 'Titoist spy' – a supporter of Josip Tito, who had enraged Stalin by becoming head of the Yugoslav government and achieving independence from Soviet control. Other offences included being an ambassador for Western imperialism, planning the restoration of capitalism and jeopardizing Hungarian independence.

The spectre of Stalin and, above all, of Beria hung over the entire proceedings. Rajik was tortured in prison, receiving the familiar specious promises of acquittal if he took responsibility for all the charges. Abuse was hurled in court, Kadar shouting: 'I say just one thing. You're not our man, you're the enemy's man. And don't you forget it! So you shouldn't have any illusions, our Party leadership is in full agreement. The question for us here is whether you're a pitiful wretch who has fallen a victim to the enemy, or whether from the moment you set foot in the workers' movement you've been an obstinate and dogged enemy of our movement. That is the only question'. Rajik eventually confessed to all the charges. The prosecution, against the earlier undertakings, called for the heaviest sentence. All 18 were executed. A succession of other trials followed, involving members of the decimated Smallholders Party.

A major player here was another sinister figure, Matyas Rakosi. He was involved in the takeover of offices, including the Ministry of the Interior,

Seen here with his liberators during the abortive Hungarian uprising, Cardinal Mindszenty is released from prison. Back in Budapest, he praised the insurgents and made a radio broadcast supporting the anti-Communist movement. But after taking refuge in the US legation, he did not escape persecution. When he was photographed saying Mass close to a US flag, he was swiftly accused of being a stooge of the Americans.

which the Smallholders Party had craved. To the latter, he declared an uncomfortable truth: 'You do not seem to realize the situation: look around in East Europe and see if you can find a country where the Ministry of the Interior is not in the hands of the Communist Party.' In 1950, it was Kador's turn to be arrested, also on charges of being a supporter of Tito. He was fortunate to escape with a three-year jail sentence, particularly as it was later estimated that 2000 people were executed and over 100,000 imprisoned.

CARDINAL JOZSEF MINDSZENTY

Arrest and trials were by no means confined to politicians. Rakosi had widened his purges beyond suspected subversives in ministries, police and municipal offices. Non-Communist organizations such as the Hungarian Catholic Youth and the Boy Scouts, previously regarded as apolitical and harmless, had been disbanded. Two days after Christmas Day 1948, police forced their way into the residence of Cardinal Jozsef Mindszenty, Hungary's most prominent religious figure. Long aware of his likely arrest, the Cardinal had previously passed an advance note to his aides, urging them to be sceptical if they heard that he had 'resigned' or 'confessed': this would be merely a sign of 'human frailty'. Earlier in the same month, he had declared in a pastoral letter:

> Mindszenty's outspoken speeches against Communism and allegations of contacts with monarchists led to charges of treason.

'Communism is an atheistic ideology. Hence by its very nature it is opposed to the spirit of the Church.' The Communists had long pursued Mindszenty for being 'at the centre of the counter-revolutionary forces in Hungary'. At the heart of the charges against him was his vocal opposition to the proposed nationalization of Hungary's 4800 Catholic schools. He had taken his campaign on tours to a spread of villages, urging people to hold on to their schools and their lands. The authorities responded by appropriating his loud-speaker truck and electric generator. He responded by urging the tolling of church bells.

In addition to the familiar practice of producing alleged confessions of guilt with forged signatures, the charges against Mindszenty of more than 40 crimes were skilfully concocted. The fact that the Church had previously accepted financial contributions from American sources was described as foreign currency abuses, while a bid to aid those who had lost their land and their churches was denounced as sabotage of land reform. Outspoken speeches against Communism, and maintaining links with members of the previous Habsburg monarchy, were both defined as treason.

Forced to discard his bishop's robe, Mindszenty endured beatings and humiliation, prefaces to hours of interrogation. But his inquisitors faced a canny opponent to whom imprisonment was nothing new. Under the Nazis, he had spent four months in jail and was aware of interrogation methods. At first, attempts to induce him to confess failed because Mindszenty kept his eating to a minimum, suspecting rightly that all his food was laced with mind-altering drugs – later, incidentally, shown to be identical to those used by the Gestapo during interrogations.

In February 1949, he went on trial. To many, the proceedings carried sinister echoes of the Moscow show trials of the 1930s, not least admissions of guilt that followed earlier declarations of innocence. Shakily, he told the court, 'I am guilty on principle and in detail of most of the accusations made'. He disowned his earlier disavowal and, when asked why he had written it, answered feebly: 'I didn't see certain things as I see them now.' The proceedings were broadcast, prompting one listener later to comment: 'This was not the voice of the strong man who had been arrested. None of those who heard his voice will ever forget the tone of his voice with which he kept repeating, "Yes, yes, that is so". It was not the voice of the real Mindszenty, but the stammering of a caricature of the man, reduced by pitiless tortures to the condition of an unresisting heap of misery.'

The verdict of life imprisonment produced worldwide condemnation, after which Mindszenty was shuffled from one prison to another until the 1956 Hungarian uprising, when he was freed briefly. After the Communists regained control, he lived under voluntary house arrest in the US legation in Budapest. Prospects were bleak for this ageing and pathetic figure, a thorn in the side of the Hungarian government, which, even with the progressive decline of Communism, regarded him as an embarrassing figure from the past. He took up residence in Vienna, where he died in 1975. With the fall of the Soviet Union, his body was brought back to Hungary for burial.

CZECHOSLOVAKIA

Following World War II, the Communist coup in Czechoslovakia ended hopes of a return to any form of democracy and paved the way for 40 years of oppressive rule. Defeat of Germany did not lessen disenchantment with the West, caused by bitter memories of the Munich Agreement of September 1938, which had ceded the German-speaking Sudetenland to Germany. Among those returning home at the war's end was one of Czechoslovakia's most popular and respected figures, Jan Masaryk, son of the country's first president Tomas Garigue Masaryk. Jan had previously served as Foreign Minister and he now regained the post in a National Front government that included the Communist Party. It was an alliance that was far from securing parity with the Soviet Union, and for Masaryk this was a homecoming to disillusion.

In 1947, Masaryk and the Communist leader Klement Gottwald were jointly summoned to Moscow by Stalin. Among other strictures, he forbade Czech participation in the Marshall Plan. This was the scheme by the US for

the reconstruction of Europe, which was seen by Stalin as a severe threat to Soviet control of Eastern Europe. Stalin's brusqueness and inflexibility led Masaryk to declare on his return: 'I left a minister of a sovereign state, but have come back as Stalin's lackey.'

DEATH OF MASARYK

In February of the next year came the Communist coup; all hope for a democratic future was swept away. The majority of Ministers resigned, in the vain belief that there would be future elections. Masaryk hung on to his job, a deeply troubled figure dreading the advent of all-powerful Communism for the Czechs and even contemplating exile. This was a prelude to the final tragedy. On 10 March 1948, Masaryk's body was discovered, barefoot and in pyjamas, beneath the bathroom window of his Foreign Office apartment in Prague's Ceminsky Palace. Many of his followers later declared that he had been murdered, on orders from Moscow. That belief was countered in 2004 by the 85-year-old Czech historian Antonin Sum, who had served as Masaryk's secretary and who firmly believed it had been a case of suicide. He declared: 'Under normal circumstances, he would never have killed himself, but he had practically no other opportunity for protest. He had to

Following the Communist coup in Czechoslovakia in February 1948, President Klement Gottwald addresses a Communist mass rally. As well as those convicted in purges, 230 death sentences were handed out, a figure that did not include those shot while trying to escape from prison camps. Many were beaten to death for minor offences.

A gesture of respect for the benefit of the cameras: on 15 March 1948, President Klement Gottwald attends the funeral of Jan Masaryk in Prague's Museum Hall.

show everyone, including the Western powers, that the Communist coup in Czechoslovakia was a bad sign for all of Europe.'

Nevertheless, many questions over the death have remained unanswered, not least why Masaryk's telephone line was later found to have been cut. If he had indeed committed suicide, why had he discussed upcoming engagements with his colleagues days before, details of which were later found in his diary? In 1993, a sensational claim was made to the Czech broadcasting service. The informant stated that a female NKVD agent, identified only as Parasinova and living in Soviet Russia, had heard her colleagues boast of murdering Masaryk by defenestration, after he had tried to flee along the window ledge. Parasinova eventually confirmed her allegations, which were intended for use in a Czech television documentary.

During an approach later made to the Russian authorities, it was revealed that Parasinova had since died. Furthermore, it was made clear that all discussion of matters and documentation concerning the Masaryk case was officially forbidden. Further revelations on the death have not been forthcoming; those who support the murder theory believe that the truth lies buried somewhere in the Soviet archives.

By the early 1950s, the Czech Communists were by no means granted an easy ride by their own supporters, particularly when it came to determining how far the state should go in emulating the Soviet Union. Predictably, the

Czechs faced Stalin-inspired purges of 'disloyal elements'. Gottwald was conscious that sparse logic accompanied Stalin's choice of victims, and as Czech President and Communist leader, he felt vulnerable. He decided to shift responsibility for disloyalty to his General Secretary, Rudolf Slansky, a long-term collaborator and friend. Slansky's name reached the NKVD. His fate was predictable: imprisonment and torture, followed by a plea of guilty to crimes against the state, accompanied by a request to be sentenced to death. Another victim was Rudolph Margolis, whose job it had been to attract vitally needed foreign trade to Czechoslovakia. Now he was deemed guilty of anti-State activities and commercial sabotage. Along with these

JAN MASARYK

Long before he became President of Czechoslovakia in 1948, Klement Gottwald set out to be a text-book Stalinist, intent on ruthlessly removing all semblance of opposition. Conciliatory overtures to Gottwald by Jan Masaryk, who had served in a coalition with the Communists, ultimately meant nothing. A Communist government was formed, following a familiar template: nationalization of the country's industry, farm collectivization, and trials for 'treason'. The trials were held at the behest of Stalin, who had sensed both a pro-American and pro-Jewish stance in the Czech government. All opposition was swept away. The trials decreed the execution of Rudolf Slansky, the party's general secretary, and Vlado Clementis, the Foreign Minister. Scores of government officials served terms of imprisonment.

Opposition to Communism and to Gottwald's rule had not been lacking – centring notably on Jan Masyrk and on Eduard Benes, the peasant's son who had served as Foreign Minister and Czechoslovkia's second president.

For many Czechs, Prague-born Masaryk was a debonair, humourous figure with a populist streak, in sharp contrast to the leaders of a drab Communist regime. When it came to opposing an existing social order, he had inspiration to hand. His father, Tomas, a self-educated coachman's son from Moravia, became the twice-elected first

president of an independent Czechoslovakia. As a member of the Vienna Parliament for 10 years, he had been a progressive voice: advocating reconciliation of all western and southern Slav groups.

At first, Jan seemed to lack his father's ambition. Keen to make his own life, he escaped to America, shunning the large mid-west Slavic community. On the eve of World War I, he returned home and was drafted into the Austro-Hungarian army. Later, he completed his studies before embarking on a diplomatic and political career. With the return of peace, he went to Washington as *Chargé d'Affaires*. By the time of his death in 1937, Jan's father was urging support for Edvard Benes, his like-minded successor, as President. Benes had joined with Tomas in a campaign to establish an independent state for the Czech people. All too soon came disaster in the form of the Munich Agreement, which ended any dreams of Czech autonomy. Benes went into voluntary exile, as head of a provisional government in London, returning home as President for three years. But he was on borrowed time: the struggle of power was won by Klement Gottwald. Benes, a broken man, resigned from office, dying three months later. The cause of Masaryk's violent death, remains a mystery but like that of so many of Stalin's opponents, it had proved remarkably convenient for those in power.

MELITA NORWOOD

In 1992, Vasili Nikitisch Mitrokhin, a former senior operative in the First Chief (Foreign intelligence) Directorate of the KGB, defected to Britain, bringing with him what the Federal Bureau of Investigation called 'The most complete and extensive intelligence ever received from any source.' It was a vast volume of material culled from thousands of top-secret files. Four years later, the British government decided that the archive should be made public and the papers were made available to Professor Christopher Andrew of the University of Cambridge. Two volumes of the material, assembled by Mitrokhin and Andrew, were published as *The Mitrokhin Archive* in 1999.

As far as the UK was concerned, one of the revelations to catch media attention was the unmasking at the age of 87 of Melita Norwood (codenamed 'Hola'), whose spying career went undetected for half a century. In Mitrokhin's opinion, Mrs Norwood 'was, on present evidence, both the most important British female agent in KGB history and the longest serving of all Soviet spies in Britain'. Through her job at the British Non-Ferrous Metals Research Association (cover for nuclear research), she had access to highly secret material in the field of metallurgy. Her Soviet case officer at this time was revealed to be Ursula Beurton ('Sonia'), which meant that 'Britain's leading female agent was thus probably run for several years by one of the few female Soviet controllers'. According to Mitrokhin's notes, she was assessed throughout her career as a 'committed, reliable and disciplined agent, striving to be of the utmost assistance'. For the 40 years that she worked for Moscow, Mrs Norwood made little money and continued to live in the same simple South London home that she had bought on marrying 50 years before. To Press interviewers, she insisted that she had served out of ideological belief not for financial reward, and that she was totally unrepentant.

charges came those of indulging in 'Trotskyite, Titoist-Zionist activities in the service of American imperialism'. All followed the pattern of accusations common in the 1950s and were calculated to appeal to nationalist and anti-Semitic sentiment, as well as to discredit all opposition.

The court sessions followed the familiar pattern of elaborate theatre: scrupulous rehearsal to eliminate any unwelcome defence or delays. There was heavy public attendance and widespread media coverage, as well as orders to the rank-and-file that they were to sign petitions for the death penalty. Of the 14 Communist leaders or bureaucrats brought to trial – 11 of them Jews – 11 were hanged and three sentenced to life imprisonment. Other trials on a smaller scale were subsequently held across the country, attracting similar penalties.

Calls for free elections and the restoration of human rights in all the countries occupied by Soviet forces fell on deaf ears. At the Potsdam conference, Stalin had made plain his intentions: 'A freely elected

government in any of these countries would be anti-Soviet, and that
we cannot allow.' It was a pledge Stalin continued to honour.

THE SOVIET ATOMIC BOMB

By the middle and late 1940s in Moscow, Stalin's health was a source of
major anxiety. The first signs of deterioration had been progressive short-
term memory loss, which increasingly meant that a number of his projects
would be left unfinished without warning. The customary stream of
instructions, issued over the dinner table or during bouts of heavy drinking,
were often confusing and contradictory. His arteriosclerosis, dating from his
early sixties, was becoming marked, along with his increasing tiredness.
There had, however, been no lessening of his ruthlessness and capriciousness
when it came to his treatment of colleagues. At the end of 1945, Stalin told
his commissars that he no longer had any confidence in Molotov, whom he
considered had devalued the prestige of state and government in the pursuit
of popularity abroad. Then had come the *coup de grâce*: 'I can no longer
consider such a comrade to be my first deputy.' Another dismissal was that of
Vsevolod Merkulov, the minister for state security, who was accused of
softness. In his place came Viktor Abakumov from SMERSH, who brought
with him to the MGB two of his toughest generals.

Yet another early obsession of Stalin's reasserted itself: gaining
supremacy for the Soviet Union in the field of atomic weaponry.

The bleak spot near
Kurchatov, Kazakhstan,
where the first Soviet
explosion of a plutonium
bomb took place on 29
August 1949. Radiation
traces are still detectable.
The area is marked by a
crater no more than
3 metres (10 ft) deep and
50 metres (165 ft) across.
Chunks of vitrified
concrete and melted steel
girders are still visible.
The US believed that the
test would not have been
possible without
information passed to the
Soviets by physicists
working in the US.

131

Following the announcement that the Soviet Union had a plutonium bomb, which was exploded on 29 August 1949, the United Nations General Assembly gathered at Flushing, New York. The US government launched a programme to develop its own hydrogen bomb.

Initiatives to develop the first atomic bomb for the Soviet Union via an espionage campaign dated way back to the war years. In 1941, the British NKVD informant John Cairncross, a former civil servant who worked for MI6 (UK Foreign Intelligence), had arranged for a telegram to be sent to Moscow 'about the contents of a most secret report of the Government Committee on the development of uranium atomic energy to produce explosive material, which was submitted on 24 September 1941 to the War Cabinet'. This report reached Beria, who alerted Moscow to the British plans for building an atomic bomb. Beria later reported that the British high command was satisfied that the theoretical problems of constructing an atomic bomb had been 'fundamentally solved' and that the cream of British scientists were collaborating on the project.

As a result, Soviet scientists began investigating the best ways of stealing a march on Britain. By 1944, Beria's role in this field had grown apace. He had been appointed Marshal of the Soviet Union and he was charged with the supervision of the entire atomic bomb project. Full use was made of

NKVD muscle. The Gulags were swept right across Russia, releasing prisoners to clear tracks of land. Those with specialist building skills constructed laboratories and attendant buildings as well as laying railway track. As for the scientists working at the Russian Federal Nuclear Centre (otherwise known as Arzamas-16), which was situated at Sarov, some 480km (300 miles) east of Moscow, deaths from the effects of radiation sickness are believed to have amounted to tens of thousands.

KLAUS FUCHS

The Soviets went talent-spotting for informants abroad. Regarded as the most important of the British atomic spies was a Communist physicist, Klaus Fuchs, a naturalized refugee from Nazi Germany, a convinced Stalinist and initially a GRU operative. Fuchs was given security clearance to work in Britain, and late in 1941 he approached the underground German Communist Party in the UK for aid in passing to the Soviets information gathered while working as a statistician at the University of Birmingham on the Tube Alloys project – the cover name for the co-ordination of atomic research. Fuchs was passed at first to Simon Davidovich Kremer, an officer in the military attaché's department at the GRU London residency, and subsequently in the summer of 1942 to Ursula Beurton.

As was the practice with spies, who were well aware that they could be discarded and betrayed if they did not deliver, demands on Fuchs were progressively stepped up. When he was selected by the British to work in collaboration with American scientists in New York, he received instructions from Anatoli Yakovlev, undercover GRU agent at the Soviet consulate in New York, to make contact with Harry Gold (real name Golodnotsky).

Gold was a long-term Soviet spy who remained Fuchs's controller throughout the two-and-a-half years that the scientist served two masters in the United States, the British and the Soviets. While working as a physicist in Los Alamos National Laboratory, Fuchs was able to pass on details of the first fission weapons and early models of the hydrogen bomb. It took until 1949 for American investigations to reveal the presence of a British traitor.

Other countries were scoured for scientists willing to be turncoats, and the first Soviet bomb was tested at Kazakhstan at 7 a.m. on 29 August 1949. An unusually benevolent Beria, in the belief that he was unassailable in prestige and power,

An ID photograph of Klaus Emil Julius Fuchs, issued while he was working at the Los Alamos National Laboratory, from where he passed information to the Soviet Union about the construction of nuclear weapons. After his release, Fuchs settled in East Germany, receiving the Order of Merit for the Fatherland and the Order of Karl Marx.

K. E. J. Fuchs

handed out lavish gifts to the chief scientific brains involved. But the benevolence was only superficial. According to one source, he had previously compiled a dossier listing each person's punishment – firing squad or Gulag – if the project had failed.

THE LENINGRAD PURGE

Two days after the test, Beria had fresh preoccupations, prompted by the death of Andrei Zhdanov, who was not only a powerful member of the Politburo but was considered by many to be Stalin's successor. Deaf to all warnings, Zhdanov had refused, even with the urging of Stalin, to control his drinking. Early health warnings were followed by a succession of heart attacks, the final collapse occurring at the party health resort at Valhi, northwest of Moscow.

Viktor Abakumov (right) followed his wartime post as leader of SMERSH by becoming head of the MGB in charge of the 'Leningrad Affair' purge. His downfall came in 1954: following the overthrow of Beria, he was executed.

VICTOR SEMIONOVICH ABAKUMOV

Anyone who had dealings with Viktor Semionovich Abakumov, the notoriously brutal head of the MGB, could attest that he was a man who revelled in the scent of blood, taking a distinct pleasure in torture. It is said that before inflicting hideous pain on a prisoner he took particular care to unroll an already heavily blood-stained carpet to cover his expensive Persian rugs.

He was born in 1908 to a hospital boilerman and a laundress and received no formal education, so he might well never have advanced beyond being a GULAG guard, a position he held after being demoted from the OGPU for scandalous behaviour. However, by the late 1930s he had managed to secure a job in the NKVD, installing surveillance equipment in the homes of suspects, as well as carrying out searches and arrests. His weaknesses, soon spotted by his superiors, were women and his willingness to accept bribes. Such qualities led him open to blackmail. Consequently, Beria reckoned he had found the ideal, biddable deputy.

Subservience, however, was far from being in Abakumov's nature: his search was on for still more power. And when Stalin, dissatisfied with Vsevolod Merkulov, the less than forcible minister at the MGB, sent for Abakumov, the latter seized the chance. He was obliged to tread carefully since he was still under Beria's supervision.

But then the familiar happened: Stalin grew suspicious and resentful of what he saw as Abakumov's excessive power and had him arrested. A handy pretext was Abakumov's lifestyle. By way of relaxing after interrogations, he was known to escape to the MGB officers' club, to be entertained by a string of mistresses in private rooms stocked with liqueurs and French perfumes. Furthermore, MGB property, crammed with china and crystal vases, was funded to build his own apartments.

Accused also of having fabricating evidence in the Leningrad case of 1946, he was confined to a refrigerated cell and shot on Stalin's instructions in December 1952.

Beria, now aligned with his old rival Georgi Malenkov, who had aided him in the 1930s purges, saw a fresh opportunity to gain power by seeking out those who had been Zhdanov's associates in Leningrad. This accorded with Stalin's mood. His jealousy of Leningrad was well established, although the city had long since ceded the seat of government to Moscow. In 1946, Zhdanov had been given the task of denouncing the city's leading writers in the general campaign against 'bourgeois formalism'. However, since the siege in World War II, Leningrad had been widely viewed as the 'hero city' and Stalin, as he approached his 70th birthday on 21 December 1949, became obsessed with the notion that its populace were craving independence. An attack was launched against those he believed were promoting free thinking.

A particular focus were those involved with the economy and business, and many were accused of establishing a wholesale trade market without the approval of Moscow. Stalin's suspicions fastened on Nicolai Voznesensky, a noted academic and a prominent organizer of the wartime economy, who was thought to be looking for fresh opportunities. Voznesensky was arrested, along with Alexei Kuznetsov, the brusque and avowedly ambitious Central Committee Secretary. Stalin went even further in his vindictiveness, ridding himself not only of Nicolai but also his brother Alexander, Rector of Leningrad University, and his sister Maria, who was alleged to have held anti-revolutionary views as far back as the 1920s. Executions and tortures were the province of Abakumov's MGB. As detailed by Simon Sebag Montefiore in *Stalin: The Court of the Red Tsar*, it was a task fulfilled enthusiastically. Kuznetsov was so badly beaten that his eardrums were perforated, while another prisoner, Turko, testified after Stalin's death that his head was smashed against a wall. The fact that a female prisoner, Zakrizhevskaya, was pregnant made no difference. Her torture came on the direct order of Abakumov, during which time she miscarried.

> Kuznetsov was so badly beaten that his eardrums were perforated, while another prisoner, Turko, had his head smashed against a wall.

By the time the Leningrad purge was completed, some 2000 had been imprisoned or exiled. The museum dedicated to the wartime siege was closed, not to be reopened for 40 years. During that, time the city's wartime history was barely acknowledged. For Stalin, a chapter had closed.

THE DOCTORS' PLOT

But Stalin's paranoia raged unchecked, characterized next by a fierce campaign of anti-Semitism. With the onset of the Cold War and the founding of Israel in 1948, Stalin considered that the threat of war lay with the United States, the arch-imperialist power with a vocal Jewish lobby and support for Zionism. At home, suspicion fastened on the Jewish Anti-Fascist Committee (JAC), which had been set up during the war to secure Jewish support abroad. It was now closed down and a concerted drive against 'cosmopolitans' – in fact, Jews – was launched. The press, predictably, was a prominent target: the Yiddish newspaper *Eynikayt* ('Unity') was forced out of business, along with *Der Emes,* the Yiddish language publishing house.

An early victim was Solomon Losovsky, a former assistant foreign minister and director of the JAC. Deemed 'crypto-Zionist', he was arrested by the MGB, held until 1952 and executed. A sinister fate awaited Solomon Mikhoels, a popular figure in Moscow's Yiddish Theatre. He had used its stage to quote a speech by the Soviet Ambassador Andrei Gromyko to the United Nations in favour of Israel's independence. On a car journey from Moscow to Minsk, he was involved in a collision with a truck and killed. To many, the role of the MGB seemed certain; staging motor accidents had long been a method employed by its predecessors. Other members of the Anti-Fascist Committee were arrested and charged with disloyalty, bourgeois nationalism and cosmopolitanism, as well as planning to set up a Jewish republic in the Crimea 'to serve US interests'. Stalin, claiming to be shocked by the sudden death of Solomon Mikhoels, allowed him an elaborate funeral that drew 10,000 mourners. The flood of arrests and torture of other members of the Committee, many of whom were later shot, soon resumed. As his physical powers declined, so did Stalin's widespread distrust of even his closest advisers, many of whom he was convinced were out to kill him.

Vladimir Vinogradov, Stalin's own personal doctor, advised him, in view of his declining health, to lessen his workload. The suggestion that his powers were waning was not to be tolerated, however. His anti-Semitism increasing, Stalin ordered the arrest of Vinogradov, along with several other doctors, some of them Jewish, at the rigidly exclusive Kremlin hospital and clinic. The clinic was regularly patrolled by the investigations branch of the MGB, where a young radiologist and insider Dr Lydia Timashuk revealed that she had treated Zhdanov before his fatal heart attack. Anxious to protect herself from any blame, she stated that she had been overruled in her treatment of Zhdanov by Dr Vinogradov, who had deliberately underrated Zhdanov's condition. Stalin was convinced of a general cover-up involving other doctors, whom he was convinced had plans to kill Kremlin leaders.

Stalin now took centre stage. Viktor Abakumov, the Minister of State Security, was dismissed on a package of convenient charges, including corruption, the misappropriation of public funds and accepting bribes.

Beria often spent weekends with Stalin and his family at his country *dacha*. In this idyllic domestic scene, Stalin reads papers in the background while his daughter Svetlana sits on Beria's lap. However, anyone craving power or who was too close to Stalin invited elimination.

Replacing him as MGB boss was Semyon Ignatiev, a pliable bureaucrat from outside the security services and a man terrified of Stalin. Suitably cowed, he was told: 'If you do not obtain confessions from the doctors, we will shorten you by a head.' The job of torturer went to a vindictive specialist, Mikhial Ryumin. Known as 'the Midget', he was by common consent one of the most repellent of those involved in what became known as the 'Doctors' Plot'.

CONSPIRACY UNCOVERED

On 13 January 1953, the world learnt that a vast conspiracy hatched by nine doctors, six of whom were Jews, had been unmasked. *Pravda*, under the headline 'Murderers in White Gowns', reported that that a number had already confessed to killing Zhdanov in 1948 and, before that, Alexsandr Shcherbakov, who had been Secretary of the Leningrad Regional Committee and who had been thought to have died of natural causes in 1945. All the medical consultants and doctors were incarcerated in the Lubyanka, some quickly confessing to killing Zhdanov, among others. The indictment also accused Vinogradov and, another defendant, Dr Meer Vovsi, of intending to poison Stalin, Beria and Malenkov.

The discrediting of the doctors was orchestrated by a concerted media campaign to whip up anti-Semitic hysteria. Jews were subjected to verbal abuse right across the country. Those suspected of being Jewish and who had hoped to conceal their ethnic origins and identities had their homes raided; their passports were seized, making it simple for the authorities to identify them. Stalin even considered promoting a scheme to have all Jews deported to a region of eastern Siberia.

The so-called 'Doctors' Plot', was, as it turned out, Stalin's last great criminal conspiracy. But it was by no means the full extent of his plans. Jews were not the only group in the line of fire. Fresh objects of suspicion were Mingrelians, members of an ethnic division of Georgia. Incidentally, this was a source of anxiety to Beria, who was himself an Mingrelian and already worried that his power base was threatened. An ominous sign was a sudden end of invitations to spend weekends at Stalin's dacha, a privilege that he had for a long time enjoyed. Then came an order that Beria must replace the Georgian staff of his household with Russians.

THE DEATH OF STALIN

Stalin died on 5 March 1953, five days after collapsing following a bibulous dinner with Beria, Malenkov, Nikita Khrushchev and Nicolai Bulganin, all of whom were contenders for the succession. On the morning of 2 March, Stalin suffered a stroke. Malenkov, Beria and the rest waited a full 24 hours before returning with doctors. Paralysis was diagnosed; it took Stalin a further three-and-a-half hours to die. Svetlana, his daughter, later wrote that 'The death agony was terrible … He literally choked to death'. Khrushchev's record during Stalin's last phase proved, in view of subsequent events, particularly illuminating: 'As soon as Stalin showed signs of consciousness, Beria threw himself on his knees, seized Stalin's hand and kissed it. When he again lost consciousness and closed his eyes, Beria stood

A French depiction of Georgi Malenkov, the future First Minister, standing over Stalin's body while his daughter Svetlana and his son Vassili grieve in the background. Little grief was felt by those intriguing for the succession.

The body of Stalin lies in state, March 1953. For over 24 hours following a period of semi-consciousness, he had been left lying on the floor in vest and pyjamas, until his death was assured.

up and spat … spewing hatred.' At the moment of Stalin's death, Beria was described by Svetlana as being 'radiant' and 'regenerated'. While the rest queued to kiss the still warm corpse, Beria strode from the room and was heard shouting for his chauffeur: 'Khrustalev, the car!'. His destination was the Kremlin.

Soon Beria was followed by the rest; inevitably, there was feverish infighting as all staked their claims to the most attractive cabinet portfolios. Few concealed their private relief at Stalin's passing. The political memoirs of Molotov, published in 1993, claim that Beria boasted to him that he had poisoned Stalin. No hard evidence has been produced to support this assertion, though many believe that additional relevant documentation lies unreleased within the Soviet archives. Beria was later blamed for the late arrival of the doctors by insisting that Stalin had been 'sleeping' rather than recognizing that he had lost consciousness. Others believe that Beria's tardiness followed agreement by all the Soviet leaders that Stalin should be allowed to die.

MALENKOV VERSUS BERIA

Malenkov, initially the most powerful man in the post-Stalinist leadership, became First Minister, but Beria, as Second Minister, began laying plans to outmanoeuvre Malenkov and seize the leadership. Beria's powers, free of the shackles of Stalinism, seemed enormous and unassailable. He commanded the political police, all external espionage, the militia with 300,000 troops, the labour camps and their inmates. He also had links to a substantial portion of Soviet industry.

Further empire-building within the security service continued apace with the merger of the MGB into the infinitely more powerful MVD (*Ministerstvo Unutrennikh Del*, Ministry of Internal Affairs) responsible for internal affairs, including secret police functions. This boosted opposition to Beria, which was already stirring, prompted by fears that his move was ultimately to place the MVD above the Party.

He had lost no time in adopting tactics to raise his public profile to discredit his rivals. Certainly, barely a month after Stalin's death, he directed that all those imprisoned in the 'Doctors' Plot' were to be released, since, in the words of an official statement, 'the bases of the charges against them of anti-terrorist and espionage activity are lacking'.

Two of those arrested had died under torture, while the survivors were mental and physical wrecks. Although this was claimed to represent a step towards greater liberalism generally, the move was also practical: the country and their leaders could ill afford to be deprived of indispensable medical talent. There was therefore general agreement that the time had come to draw a line under the 'Doctors' Plot'. Ryumin, who had already been sacked by an impatient Stalin and demoted to an obscure desk job, was arrested and later executed.

In agreement with Khrushchev and Malenkov, Beria put an end to the anti-Semitic witch-hunt. A statement by *Pravda* completely reversed Stalin's

Stalin's body is carried to the Hall of Columns, House of Unions in Moscow, following the lying in state on 10 March 1953. To the extreme right of the picture is Lavrenti Beria, inscrutable now but exultant at the time of Stalin's death, believing he would accede to power. Nikita Khruschev, who engineered Beria's downfall, recalled: 'To put it crudely, he had a housewarming over Stalin's corpse before it was in his coffin.'

Barely three months after the death of Stalin, 10,000 workers in East Berlin erupted onto the streets and could not be controlled, action that was largely due to Beria's mistake in weakening the power of the MVD. He faced severe criticism for blaming the crisis on the East German authorities. The fear in Moscow was that the supremacy of Communist rule in Eastern Europe would be severely undermined by the demonstrations.

intentions, denouncing provocateurs in the former MGB for igniting 'nationalist dissension and undermining the unity of the Soviet people which had been welded together by internationalism'.

This however was far from being as conciliatory as it seemed. As co-author of *KGB: The Inside Story of its Foreign Operations*, Oleg Gordievsky, one of the foremost Soviet defectors of the Cold War, revealed: '... Though the crude anti-Semitism of Stalin's final years ceased, belief in a Zionist conspiracy continued. The MVD, and later the KGB, took back none of the Jewish officers purged in the early 1950s, and maintained a total ban on Jewish entrants.'

THE FALL OF BERIA

The death of Stalin created a vacuum, not only in the Soviet Union, but internationally. Beria lost no time in moving to strengthen control over both sectors in his security empire. Praesidium members, only too aware that he held potentially embarrassing dossiers on most of them, were at first slow to move. Armed with fresh confidence, Beria proceeded to install a loyal MVD henchman as the new head of the Foreign Directorate, Lieutenant-Colonel Vasili Stepanovich Ryasoy, a man who was later said to lack experience in foreign intelligence and to be Beria's lackey. Ryasoy's instructions were to summon a group of Residents (party representatives) from a number of countries for discussions in Moscow on future policy. This proved to be a miscalculation: the main effect was to identify them to Kremlin-watchers in the West and blow their covers.

Worse followed. On 17 June 1953, violence erupted among discontented workers in East Berlin, previously unheard of since the MVD had proven expert in crushing any signs of dissent. In the belief that the bulky intelligence apparatus in the German Democratic Republic (GDR) needed a fundamental overhaul, Beria recalled some 800 MVD personnel. Entire departments were thrown into chaos. Protests at demands for increases in production quotas quickly escalated into lightning strikes, which included calls for free elections.Soviet tanks were attacked by stone-throwing mobs. To the dismay of observers in Moscow, graphic images and reports were carried by newspapers in the West. Far more worrying were fears that similar uprisings would break out in the other Communist satellites.

Beria flew to Berlin to assess the situation. His suspicions were aroused when he heard that the Praesidium was gathering at an unusual hour, but he was assured that there was no need for him to attend. This was enough to send him home immediately. The mood he encountered was arctic. He was accused of helping to bring about the first serious challenge to Communist rule in the Soviet bloc, jeopardizing Party rule, Russian dominance and the integrity of its Eastern-European empire. His reaction to the accusation of mismanagement over East Berlin was to shift the blame to the GDR itself, which he declared could be kept in check only by the presence of Soviet troops. The future Foreign Minister Andrei Gromyko, present as an observer, declared that Beria spoke 'in a dismissive tone and with a sneer on his face'.

> Beria's moves to strengthen the security of his empire seriously misfired and he was stripped of all offices.

ARMY COUP

In the face of such arrogance, the movement to overthrow him gained momentum. Zhukov and Khrushchev, the main instigators, reasoned that they were hardly likely to secure the support of Beria's police units. These had become increasingly powerful – even to the extent, it was widely believed, of bugging the telephones of close colleagues. The most profitable area for the two conspirators was plainly the army, many of whose senior figures were keen to avenge colleagues purged by Beria. Zhukov set out to canvass its senior ranks through Bulganin, as Minister of Defence. For Khrushchev, one of the main stumbling blocks was the First Minister, Malenkov, but he was eventually won over, along with Sergei Kruglov, one of Beria's deputies.

The scene was set for the crucial Praesidium meeting of 26 June, which Khrushchev later claimed to have attended with a gun in his pocket.

> In the early 1980s human bones, possibly from some of his victims, were unearthed during construction work near Beria's home in Moscow.

According to his account, Beria asked: 'Well, what's on the agenda today. Why have we met so unexpectedly?' At this point, Malenkov was scheduled to speak, but his nerve failed him. Khrushchev took over, declaring that there was only one item on the agenda: 'the anti-Party, divisive activity of imperialist agent Beria'. Then followed the proposal that Beria should be dropped from the Praesidium and from the Central Committee, and expelled from the Party, followed by handover to the Court Martial. In turn he was denounced by Molotov and Bulganin. In response to the pressing of a concealed button by Malenkov, Beria was seized by Zhukov, who entered at the head of a group of armed officers.

A tank and motor rifle division formed a ring around the Kremlin, their strength ensuring that any response by the MVD would be no match for them. In addition, 50 armed guards were posted outside the Kremlin's Borovitskie Gates, moving in to take possession of their prisoner. On the stroke of midnight, a black government car, its light flashing, streaked out of the Kremlin; the guards forced Beria to kneel on the floor. In the bunker beneath Osipenko Street in central Moscow was a 20-metre (65-foot) square cell without windows and bare except for a wooden bed, two tables and a chair. The light was kept on at all times.

As if to underline his ascendancy, Khrushchev, who had emerged as the leader of the coup, delayed telling the MVD officially of Beria's arrest. In his book, Oleg Gordievsky recalls that as a 14-year-old on holiday in the Ukraine, he received a letter from his father, a colonel in the NKVD, telling him: 'There was a sensational event yesterday. Portraits of the boss were taken from the walls.' Shorn of his arrogance and with only his sycophancy still intact, Beria wrote a series of pleading letters to his former colleagues, pleading to be spared his life and asking them to find 'the smallest job for me … You will see that in two or three years I'll have straightened out fine and will still be useful to you … I ask the comrades to forgive me for writing somewhat disjointedly and badly because of my condition, and also because of the poor lighting and not having my pince-nez'.

BERIA ON TRIAL

On 14 December Beria and his co-defendants were found guilty by the Supreme Court of what had been a blandly composed indictment: 'to revive capitalism and to restore the rule of the bourgeoisie.' In no way can it be said that Beria's victims were now publicly avenged. His responsibility for countless murders was not mentioned, since that would have tarnished the image of the regime. There was, however a coded reference to his perverted sexuality: 'Crimes which testify to his moral degradation.' The Supreme Court learnt that one of the guards had found a small piece of paper with the names and addresses of four women who had been dragged to Beria's home, then raped and most likely murdered. An additional charge of working for British intelligence arose out of his 'secret connections with Foreign Intelligence until the moment of his arrest', but no firm evidence was brought to particularly indicate British involvement.

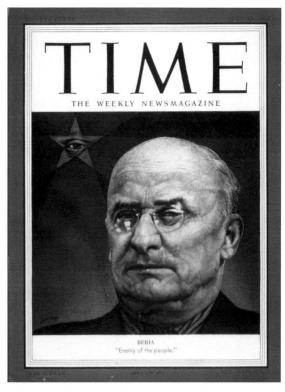

BERIA
"Enemy of the people."

Details of Beria's execution have emerged from the release of KGB archives, but some are contradictory. There appears to be general agreement, however, that he faced his last moments with dignity. He was forced to don a black suit for death and his mouth was stuffed with a bandage or towel, meaning that he was unable to make a final statement. General Batissky, who had guarded Beria for six months, sent the first of a succession of bullets into Beria's forehead. The body was wrapped in a tarpaulin, taken to a crematorium and stuffed into the flames through a hatch.

In true Stalinist tradition, Beria became a non-person; 'advice' given to subscribers to the *Great Soviet Encyclopaedia* was that they should remove his entry and insert a replacement article on the Bering Sea instead.

At the same time, there were sweeping changes. The *Politburo* was determined that never again would a state security organization be allowed to grow independently and unfettered. In pursuit of this, the right to conduct summary trials and mete out sentences became the responsibility of the Ministry of Justice. Control of police, clandestine operations, border patrols and internal security remained, broadly speaking, where they were but answerable to a new organ of state security. This was the *Komitet Gosudarstvennoy Bezopastni*, the Soviet Security and Intelligence Service, otherwise known as the KGB.

The news of Beria's downfall and death on 23 December 1953 was international news. On the cover of *Time* magazine his picture is captioned 'Enemy of the People'.

CHAPTER 8

THE KGB

Created in 1954 following the death of Stalin, the KGB quickly became the world's largest security enterprise, with the ability to effectively project the interests of the Soviet Union into every corner of the world.

T he KGB, created in March 1954 and lasting for the next 37 years, became the world's largest security enterprise. By 1980, John McMahon, deputy director for CIA Operations, stated: 'The Soviets have established a world-wide network of agents, organizations, and technical facilities to implement its programmes. That network is second to none in comparison to the major world powers in its size and effectiveness.'

Aside from its international role, the KGB held sway over more than 64,000km (40,000 miles) of the Soviet Union's sea and land frontiers. From its ornate rococo headquarters in Moscow's Dzerzhinsky Square, agents were sent to penetrate deep into the respective ministries responsible for education, science and medicine. As KGB power increased, so did its vast sprawl of official buildings. Training centres for spies were also set up in Leningrad and other towns and cities.

GLAVLIT

The grip of the censor was firm, and GLAVLIT (*Glavnoe upravlenie po delam literatury i izdatv* – the Chief Administration for Safeguarding State Secrets in Print), despatched operatives to scan newspapers, journals, and every other form of printed material. For the ordinary Russian, George Orwell's totalitarian vision, outlined in his novel *Nineteen Eighty-Four*,

Opposite: A cell door that has survived from the days of the KGB. Such exhibits are to be found in KGB museums located in a number of Russian towns and cities.

A classic Stalinist in ruthlessness and brutality, Ivan Serov was the KGB's first chief, and one of the most repressive figures of the Hungarian uprising.

came all too close to reality. Only on reaching the age of sixteen was a Soviet citizen entitled to an internal passport, and without it movement from one part of the country to another was illegal. Moreover, all passports were stamped to record their holders' movements. Agents lurked in cities, towns and villages, and no-one was immune to their investigations. Any behaviour that could be interpreted as disloyalty was punished by internment in the labour camps. The workplace was no safe refuge, either: the politically unreliable were dismissed and, after a month of unemployment, imprisoned.

THE INVASION OF HUNGARY

The first chief of the KGB was the same tough, brutal Ivan Serov who, as Beria's deputy, had carried out the mass arrests in Poland at the time of the Warsaw Rising. When the Communist take-over of Poland was well under way, Serov, with the rank of General, made his way in the spring of 1945 to East Berlin. It was from here, in the German Democratic Republic (GDR), that the *Stasi* (*Ministerium fur Staatssicherheit* – Ministry for State Security) would eventually operate. With its powerful presence, the KGB operated from the district of Karlshorst, becoming the largest base outside the Soviet Union for espionage targeted against the West as a whole. There, heavily guarded by police, Serov presided over activities that amounted to a rehearsal for the work of KGB: monitoring political parties, churches and trade unions.

From his Karlshorst base, Serov was tasked to deal with those Communist states that were considered to have strayed from the official Moscow line and which needed strong persuasion to return to 'normalization' and 'orthodoxy'. In October 1956, Hungary was presenting fresh problems, the people daringly defiant after Khrushchev's 'secret speech' in February to the Soviet 20th Party Congress, in which he had denounced Stalin's 'cult of personality'. To the West, Hungary, a country in absolute subjugation to the Soviet Union, embodied everything that the Cold War represented. Stalin's death as yet had altered nothing, and the sure consequence of any challenge to Moscow was underlined by the presence of thousands of heavily armed Soviet troops.

Even so, Hungarians dared to raise a challenge, particularly to Matyas Rakosi (1892–1971), the embodiment of self-promoting authoritarian rule. In Budapest, mass demonstrations called for the withdrawal of Soviet troops and the holding of free elections. To counter this widespread discontent, Khrushchev forced Rakosi to surrender the office of Prime Minister. After a brief tenure by another hardliner Erno Gero, the position went to Imre Nagy (1896–1958), a former Speaker of the Hungarian Parliament, who favoured a more liberal stance. Nagy was afforded strictly limited power; his deputy was Janos Kadar, a KGB puppet. During his brief tenure, Nagy attempted to maintain stability by suggesting amnesty for demonstrators, abolition of the one-party system and the withdrawal of Soviet troops.

Imre Nagy, Hungary's leader on two occasions. Here seen addressing the Parliament, he expressed the country's hope for increasingly liberal rule. On Nagy's right is his predecessor Matyas Rakosi, who had been removed from the post due to fierce popular opposition as well as Hungary's worsening economic plight.

Such proposals were anathema to Serov, who raced to Budapest on 23 October, the day of Nagy's appointment. At an emergency meeting of security officials and police, Serov demanded to know why the 'fascist and imperialist' protesters had not been fired upon. Sandor Kopacsi, the Budapest chief of police who ended up siding with the dissidents, had the courage to point out that many of the demonstrators were the young intelligentsia, the middle class and workers, who considered that they were fighting for their human rights. A quarter of a century later, Kopacsi was to recall the long, searching glare of Serov's steel-blue eyes and, above all, his threat: 'I'll have you hanged from the highest tree in Budapest!'

> Soviet tanks in Budapest fired on protesters in Parliament Square, causing some dozen deaths and an estimated 150 wounded.

Just two days after Serov's arrival, Soviet tanks, already in Budapest, fired on protesters in Parliament Square, causing some dozen deaths and an estimated 150 wounded. The people's response was fierce: Communist leaders were hanged from trees. However, five divisions of the Red Army, under the overall control of Colonel-General K Greennik of the KGB, were now approaching the Hungarian border with the intention of suppressing the rising.

Serov was not alone in seeing the situation in Hungary as likely to provide an opportunity to enhance his career. On hand also was Yuri Vladimir Andropov (1914–84), the future KGB Chairman and Soviet leader. As Ambassador to Hungary, his initial role was to assure Nagy that there was no call for worry: troop withdrawals were going ahead, he insisted, and those forces entering Hungary were merely securing free passage for those who were leaving.

TANK INVASION

Nagy was trusting enough to believe him. Thus encouraged, he announced Hungary's withdrawal from the Warsaw Pact, the military organization of Central and Eastern European Communist states, which had been set up just a year earlier to counter a possible threat from NATO. Declaring itself neutral, the country protested to the United Nations about the re-entry of Soviet troops. Andropov maintained his assurances, anxious to imply that he was open to negotiations. But all the while, plans were being hatched for the overthrow of Nagy's coalition government, a prospect that was brought nearer by Kadar, the ultimate opportunist, setting up a rival government to the east of Hungary, his power buttressed by the presence of Soviet tanks. An invitation to talks at military headquarters, ostensibly to discuss the troop withdrawals, was conveyed to Major General Pal Maleter, the Hungarian defence minister and his staff. To lull any suspicions, a lavish banquet was arranged. It was a carefully designed trap.

Serov's moment came at midnight while toasts were being drunk. Brandishing a Mauser pistol and flanked by KGB officers, he burst into the room, seizing Maleter and his entire party. On 3 November at 4 a.m., the Soviet invasion began, with the seizure of Hungary's airfields and main highway junctions. Demonstrators in the centre of Budapest were fired on, many of the wounded being tied to tanks and driven through the streets as a warning to others. Flight was patently impossible for anyone; Nagy and several of his ministers sought refuge in the Yugoslav embassy. Others, unable to do so, were arrested as 'counter-revolutionaries', among them Sandor Kopacsi, the Budapest police chief to whom Serov revealed his true identity as Chairman of the KGB.

Soviet tanks on the streets of Budapest fired on crowds, trying to stem the uprising. The KGB was on hand not only to control the Red Army troops but to take prisoners declared to be 'counter-revolutionaries'.

DOUBLE-CROSSED

On 21 November, Janos Kadar, now head of the new Soviet-backed government, gave assurances to Nagy and the other refugees in the Yugoslav embassy that they could proceed to their homes unmolested. But when they

left the embassy, Soviet officers forced their way onto the party's departing bus, seizing the passengers, who were then handed over to the KGB. Charges condemned 'The Counter-Revolutionary Conspiracy of Imre Nagy and his accomplices'. Nagy was declared the willing accomplice of Imperialism, 'principal organiser of the Counter Revolution'. After a secret trial, both Maleter and Nagy were shot – the latter for treason on 16 June 1958. Another minister died at the hands of his torturers and a second, on hunger strike, was strangled. Three years of repression and consolidation lay ahead under Kadar's puppet government.

MARKUS WOLF

For a while at least, the KGB could reckon with justification that it had won the day, and it was amply equipped to spread its work. An industrious servant was Markus Johannes ('Mischa') Wolf, who at the time had a high profile role in the East Germany HVA (*Hauptverwaltung Aufklarrung* – Department of Reconnaissance of the *Stasi*). Wolf, son of a well-known Communist writer who had fled to Moscow after the rise of Hitler, was only 29 when he took over the service, incurring criticism at first from those who considered that he was too young as well as needlessly reckless. However, Wolf had lived in Russia and spoke the language fluently. He also possessed a two-volume archive that had been seized by the Red Army, containing *Wehrmacht*, SS and Nazi records. These he proposed to use to damn those surviving West German figures with Nazi links. They could be threatened with blackmail or, in return for Wolf's silence, be persuaded to defect to the HVA, which in practice meant to its parent, the KGB.

Willy Brandt, who became West German Chancellor, was accused by the East German spymaster Markus Wolf of having betrayed prominent Communists to the *Gestapo*.

One dossier held by the East Germans was that of Reinhard Gehlen (1902–79), who had been a Major General in the *Wehrmacht* as well as chief intelligence gatherer on the Eastern Front. He was recruited subsequently by the US military to set up a spy ring directed against the Soviet Union. Vasily Mitrokhin reveals that in a move to enhance Gehlen's file, 'an additional, highly discreditable' chapter, together with other forgeries were added by Abteilung X, the HVA's active measure departments.

BRANDT UNDER ATTACK

Wolf was soon after bigger fry for character assassination and saw a likely prospect in the Lubeck-born left-wing politician Willy Brandt (1913–92). His KGB files contained thoroughly suspect material alleging that Brandt had betrayed known Trotskyites and Marxists to the *Gestapo* during World War II. The dossier also went beyond credibility: Brandt was denounced as having

The former East German spy chief Markus Wolf, seen here with his wife Andrea, giving a public reading from his book *Die Troika*, published simultaneously in a united Germany in 1989. The book, recalling the days when espionage consisted of moles and dead-letter drops, put on record Wolf's dislike of Stalin and his welcome for the age of Gorbachev's *glasnost*. After the collapse of the German Democratic Republic, Wolf was charged and sentenced for espionage, bribery and treason, but that conviction was later overturned and he received a suspended sentence on other charges.

collaborated with the CIA and the UK's SIS (Secret Intelligence Service, also known as MI6). The allegations, however unlikely, proved useful to Wolf, who intended to use them to discredit Brandt from the moment that the future Chancellor became Burgermeister of Berlin, in October 1957.

Wolf's next move was to seek out one of his most trusted agents, Gunther Guillaume, a retired East German doctor, whom Brandt had known during the war. Under instruction, Guillaume wrote to Brandt, who was then West Berlin's Mayor, pleading help for his son who was suffering persecution. Although the mere fact that Guillaume was living in the GDR should have

West German Chancellor Willy Brandt in November 1972. On the left is political aide Gunther Guillaume, the spy from the German Democratic Republic who, along with his wife Christel, penetrated Brandt's office under KGB control.

aroused the suspicions of the security services, Brandt agreed to help; Guillaume and his wife Christel quit East Berlin, and, securing jobs, settled in the Federal Republic. Both professed strong support for the SPD, the left-wing party that led a coalition under Brandt as Chancellor. All the while, the couple continued to serve their real master: both were HVA operatives.

Within three weeks of Brandt securing the Chancellorship, Guillaume had secured a job in his office. Podgy and steel-spectacled, he appeared to those who worked with him to be the ultimate bureaucrat, hard-working and pedantic. Rising from the role of mere clerk, he became one of the three personal assistants to the Federal Chancellor. One of his duties was to read and copy the important papers that crossed his desk. These included a communication from US President Richard Nixon, which outlined his plans for reshaping NATO, and, more crucially, details of Brandt's plans for negotiating with the East Germans, revealing the concessions he was willing to make. Using his wife as a courier, Guillaume passed the material either via clandestine locations or by direct delivery to a KGB controller.

Routine surveillance of Guillaume over his four years with Brandt veered from the perfunctory to the incompetent. West German intelligence acted only after being contacted by a Soviet defector who had been on a course with Guillaume at the Kiev military academy and who had been astonished to see him shown on television in the company of Brandt. From then on, West German security embarked on an elaborate double game. Guillaume was allowed to remain for a further year on the Bonn staff, a breathing space which allowed his contacts to be traced. He was given access to certain selected papers and was even allowed to accompany the Brandts to Norway for a holiday in the summer of 1973. The bluff gave the couple a false sense of security; only in April of the following year were the authorities ready to close in. A Federal Court sentenced Gunther Guillaume to 13 years' imprisonment, but he served barely half before being repatriated to East Germany in 1982. West Germany was able to exact a price, though: a number of political prisoners and alleged West German agents had to be released in exchange.

Responsibility fell on the Chancellor for a grotesque security lapse that had allowed East German intelligence to plant an agent in the higher reaches of his personal staff. In May 1974, Willy Brandt accepted full blame and resigned from the office of Federal Chancellor. His departure was greeted with relief by elements in East Germany, who had been alarmed at the aims of *Ostpolitik,* Brandt's proposals for closer relations with the West, which had always refused to recognize the GDR as a sovereign state.

IGOR GOUZENKO

As well as seeking new sources of power, the KGB received instructions from Moscow to track down dissidents and traitors, in operations often lasting for years. A striking example was provided by the case of Igor Sergeyevich Gouzenko (1919–82), a defector and a former cipher clerk in the Soviet Embassy in Ottawa. His appearances on Canadian television earned him the identity of 'the man without a face', since he always appeared with a white cloth draped over his head. Additionally, Gouzenko underwent plastic surgery and spoke in public only through a device to distort his voice.

All this was far from being melodramatic self-advertisement; Gouzenko had abundant reason for caution. The KGB had him as a marked man, going back to 5 September 1945, when he secretly stuffed more than 100 classified documents under his shirt and set out to defect, prompted by growing disenchantment with Communism and what he had gathered about the quality of life in his homeland. A further motivation was the fact that he and his family were due to be sent home. Defection, however, proved a lot harder than he had imagined. A cautious Ministry of Justice was reluctant to move against the Soviets, their allies in the World War that had only recently ended, and it refused to study the documents.

Opposite: Soviet espionage activities in Canada and the US were at their height in the early months of 1956. Public interest centred particularly on convinced Communist spy David Greenglass (far left of the picture). He testified against his fellow conspirators, the Rosenbergs, leading to their conviction and execution. Here, Greenglass is seen in the presence of Harry Gold (fifth from left), who had been spying for the Soviet Union since 1935. Both Greenglass and Gold appeared before the Senate Internal Security Subcommittee in Washington, probing Soviet spying.

Quite unwittingly, Gouzenko had chosen an inopportune moment: Canada was due to meet the Soviets, Britain, France and the United States to discuss a post-war settlement. The last thing the Canadian government wanted was anything that might develop into an espionage scandal. Gouzenko also approached a leading newspaper, which likewise expressed scant interest, thereby incidentally losing what would have been the spy scoop of the decade. Conscious that it was only a matter of time before his former colleagues discovered his duplicity, Gouzenko raced home, installing his family in an apartment opposite for the night. His fears were fully justified; all too soon he was watching through a keyhole as GRU agents broke into his apartment and started searching.

Only then was Gouzenko taken seriously by the ultra-cautious authorities, who suspected him of being a plant by the Communists and who had even contemplated returning him to Moscow. A close study of his haul revealed otherwise and proved sensational. Placed firmly in the frame as a leading GRU operative and thinly disguised Soviet military attaché in Ottawa was Colonel Nikolai Zabotin. His main task was nothing less than running one of the key networks that was probing the Allied atomic bomb programme.

ALAN NUNN MAY

One of Zabotin's senior agents was the UK physicist Alan Nunn May, who in the 1940s had been working on atomic research in Cambridge's Atomic Research Laboratory. Its work had been moved to Canada for greater wartime security and to make for easier co-operation with the Americans. His Communist sympathies soon attracted Colonel Zabotin, who passed him to a GRU lieutenant, Pavel Angelov. Nunn May was instructed to pass over information about atomic energy and uranium. Before long, he was persuaded to report on the first A-bomb trial being held in New Mexico and to supply a sample of Uranium 235.

Nunn May, who was arrested following his recall to London, was not the only Soviet agent to be exposed. Besides Klaus Fuchs and his contact Harry Gold, there was David Greenglass. Enlisted in the US Army, he was a known Communist who had been assigned to Los Alamos, where the plutonium device dropped on Nagasaki in 1945 had been developed. According to Harry Gold, Greenglass passed important information about the project to the Soviets. A trawl through Greenglass's contacts led the authorities to one Julius Rosenberg, a machinist at Los Alamos who was also a known recruiting agent for the Party. Indeed, one of his successes was Greenglass, his brother-in-law. In court, it was revealed that Julius Rosenberg, encouraged by his wife Ethel, had not only talent-spotted likely traitors but had also done everything in his power to provide top class espionage material to the Soviets. The couple were condemned to death and went to the electric chair. Gold and Greenglass drew heavy prisoner sentences. Nor were they the

only ones to be caught in the net of Canadian Intelligence. A further 39 suspects were arrested, of which 18 were eventually convicted.

A key figure on the Soviet side was Anotoli Yatskov, whose cover while working as the Rosenbergs' controller had been the role of Consul General of the Soviet Union. At the time of the trials, Yatskov took advantage of diplomatic immunity to leave Canada. In an interview in the 1990s, he claimed that the FBI had uncovered 'less than half of his network', adding with some relish that a major figure at that time had gone undetected and was still alive.

With some justification, Gouzenko believed that the KGB would shadow him to the grave. In 1975, KGB agents discovered his friendship with Thomas Cossit, a member of parliament, and deduced that Gouzenko was living in his constituency. Mitrokhin's findings reveal that Mikhail Nikolayevich Khvatov, a KGB officer stationed in Ottawa, set out to contact

Masses of demonstrators made their way to New York on 18 June 1954 to protest against the death sentences passed on Julius and Ethel Rosenberg. There was widespread belief that the couple were guilty only of low-grade espionage. But Rosenberg, a hardline Stalinist militant, had channelled significant information through the Soviet consulate.

Cossit in the hope of tracing Gouzenko's whereabouts. When that failed, Khvatov delved into the politician's background in the hope of finding information that might discredit him and provide useful for blackmail. That failed also: Cossit died in 1982. As for Gouzenko himself, he and his family were thoroughly debriefed, then given another identity by the Canadian government and settled into middle-class anonymity. This was successfully maintained until Gouzenko's death from heart failure in 1982. The KGB had failed to catch their quarry.

THE PORTLAND RING

Concern over the Gouzenko affair stretched far beyond Canada and the United States, not least within NKVD circles. Particularly interested in London had been Harold Adrian Russell ('Kim') Philby (1912–88), not only head of SIS Section IX (Soviet Counter Intelligence) but a Soviet agent who had been drawn to Communism as far back as the 1930s. Thanks to US translations of Soviet cables decrypted by what became known as the Venona Project, it was later revealed that Philby had been kept well informed of Gouzenko's debriefing. Philby reported 'an intensification of counter measures' against Soviet espionage in London. Moscow's response had been to order tight security procedures to ensure that 'the valuable agent network is protected from compromise'. Agents were told, for the moment at least, to lie low: 'Warn all our comrades to make a thorough check when going out to a meeting, and if surveillance is observed, not to attempt under any circumstances to evade the surveillance and meet the agent …'

Ruislip, a sedate, west of London suburb, was an improbable setting for one of the most sensational KGB operations outside the United States and the Continent. Peter Kroger, an antiquarian bookseller, and his wife Helen, both Canadians, had settled there in the 1950s, seemingly doing little beyond socializing with their immediate neighbours, the Searchs. Occasionally, the Krogers were accompanied by Gordon Lonsdale, introduced to neighbours as their 'young Canadian friend'. There was no reason to suppose that the Krogers were anything more than what they appeared to be: a sociable couple perfectly content with a quiet suburban life. However, it was an elaborately staged deception. The Krogers – in fact an American couple named Morris and Lona Cohen – played their role well. Hardly surprising, since they were seasoned KGB agents, who were well versed in undercover operations, having worked with the Rosenbergs and their circle.

A full ten years after his defection, Ivor Gouzenko still feared the KGB. Here, in October 1954 in Toronto, Canada, he was interviewed by a journalist and talked to other reporters in a disguised voice. With the Cold War remaining a reality, Gouzenko expressed a wildly held belief that any professed soft line by the Soviet Union might still preface an attack on the United States.

Ethel Gee in 1970, returning to her home in Portland, Dorset, western England. She had served nine years in prison for her part in the Soviet spy ring. In sentencing Ethel, the Lord Chief Justice had stated: "I am inclined to think that yours was the strongest character of the two. I think you acted from greed."

A telephone call to the Searchs from the local police provided the first sign that their cover was compromised. This was followed by a visit from the quietly courteous Jim Skardon, one of MI5's most efficient agents. To the bewildered Searchs, Skardon explained that matters of national security were involved and requested 'permission' to install watchers in their house, which included a room overlooking the Krogers' bungalow. The Searchs, keen on their privacy, protested. Skardon, his mild manner intact throughout, made it clear that their 'permission' did not enter into it; he had the full backing of the law.

MICHAL GOLENIEWSKI

The trail began in Washington after Michal Goleniewski, a Polish defector and former intelligence officer, reported the existence of a British naval spy for the KGB who had once worked at the British Embassy in Warsaw. It did not take long for British intelligence to identify him as Harry Houghton (codename SHAH). A one-time chief petty officer, he had been based in

Poland, where he had been active in the black market. He was sent back to England before his tour of duty had ended, but this had not prevented him from securing a job at the British Admiralty's Under-Water Weapons Establishment at Portland on the south coast. There, as his marriage to his wife Peggy came under progressive strain, he met Ethel ('Bunty') Gee, a blacksmith's daughter who became his mistress.

An old contact in Poland, who was well aware of Houghton's weakness for luxuries, suggested to him that he might procure for himself a useful source of additional income by contacting Gordon Lonsdale. Houghton was led to believe that this prosperous well-dressed extrovert had a secure job as a US Navy Commander at the Embassy in London. This proved an ingenious cover for the Russian Konon Trofimovich Molodi, who had been carefully groomed by the KGB for life in Britain with the aim of controlling what became known as the 'Portland Ring'. It was proposed that Houghton should adopt a central role in providing information. This was to reach Moscow via the Krogers; as was to be revealed, they possessed thoroughly efficient resources. The weakness in the chain, however, was Houghton himself, who attracted suspicion by becoming addicted to a lifestyle that should have been

THE VENONA PROJECT

In the forefront of the ongoing espionage war between the Soviet Union and the United States was a highly secretive programme codenamed Venona. This employed the foremost cryptographic talent within the US's National Security Agency at Langley, Virginia. Originally created in 1943 to intercept any Nazi-Soviet peace talks at the end of World War II, Venona was upgraded subsequently to decipher any messages from a string of countries making contact with Moscow. It proved a massive task, for there were no less than five different systems of codes involved, with the focus on those relating to the KGB and the GRU.

The entire Venona operation attracted some of America's brightest linguistic talents, notably the formidable duo of Meredith Gardner, a scientist with a mastery of six languages and their codes, and Robert Lamphere, who joined the project in 1948 as the liason and case controller for the Federal Bureau of Investigation (FBI). Both messages to be passed to the Bureau's Chief

J Edgar Hoover, prompting investigations of suspected spies.

At the hub of the KGB – and thus a rich source of information for Venona – was its Second Chief Directorate, which handled international counterintelligence and security and controlled SMERSH ("Death to Spies"). Details of the innermost workings of the KGB's methods formed much of the harvest for Venona, including the countermeasures taken against FBI surveillance, the detection of bugging devices and the means of ensuring the loyalty of agents.

Venona also kept tabs on Soviet methods of recruiting American Communists for espionage. Perhaps its biggest coup was learning how the KGB possessed large formations of police troops, prison camp guards and a small army to protect Stalin and the Soviet leadership. Throughout the cold war, the very existence of Venona, which ran until 1980, remained classified, and to this day many of its findings have not been released.

way beyond his means. A Portland security officer observed him running an expensive car with Gee and being free with cash in neighbourhood bars. Furthermore, his estranged wife Peggy came across a bundle of naval papers in their home. It was time for MI5 and Scotland Yard's Special Branch to act.

Their most important arrests came near London's Old Vic Theatre, where they seized Houghton and Bunty Gee in the act of handing over to Lonsdale a shopping basket containing four Admiralty files and undeveloped film in a sealed tin. British Intelligence now had in its possession some 300 photographs of naval stores and equipment, including details of the nuclear submarine HMS *Dreadnought*. These arrests were followed by Special Branch and the police swooping down on the Krogers. The two were subjected to vigorous grilling, especially about their links with Lonsdale, then arrested. Helen Kroger asked if she could be allowed to stoke the boiler before leaving – a ruse unlikely to be swallowed by an experienced woman police officer, who insisted on going through Helen's handbag first. Inside, she found an envelope containing a letter in Russian, together with a sheet of paper with typed black numbers in code: grid references to a map that showed locations for meeting places.

> Greville Wynne and Gerald Brooke were both pawns in the game of KGB espionage exchange.

Peter Wright, Assistant Director of MI5 and a central figure in Britain's relentless drive to detect Soviet espionage, wrote in his memoirs *Spy Catcher*: 'The most interesting find of all was a signal plan for special high-speed transmissions from Moscow. Hidden in a cookery jar we found a bottle of magnetic iron oxide used to print out the Morse from the high-speed message onto a tape so that it could be read without being transferred onto a sophisticated tape recorder and slowed down. It was a new technique, and explained why we had failed to detect any transmissions to the Kroger house in the months before the arrests. … We searched the house for nine days. On the last day we located the transmitter. It was hidden in a cavity under the kitchen floor, along with cameras and other radio equipment. Everything was carefully concealed in moisture-resistant sealed packages, and the whole system had obviously been designed to be stored for a considerable length of time'. The search also unearthed thousands of pounds, dollars and travellers' cheques and seven passports.

EXPOSED

At the home of Bunty Gee, whose weekly wage at Portland was £10, cash amounting to around £4000 was discovered. At Houghton's house a number of navigational charts were unearthed, together with a plan of nearby Admiralty property. Other finds were a wireless set in the living room capable of receiving transmissions from around the world, together with a

Spy centre in suburbia: a converted radiogram, together with recorder and headset able to receive three types of high speed transmissions from Moscow. It was unearthed in the bungalow occupied by the Krogers, central figures in the Portland Spy Ring. Britain's security services attempted in vain to maintain a media blackout so that news of the discovery would not reach the Soviets. But, within hours, reporters and photographers besieged the bungalow and a major espionage coup was revealed.

false-bottomed cigarette lighter, torches with hollow batteries and flasks fitted with secret containers.

All five of those involved pleaded not guilty to the charge that between 14 April 1960 and 7 January 1961 they had conspired to break the British Official Secrets Act. Houghton and Gee were each sentenced to 15 years in prison; both served 10 years. As far as Russia and the KGB were concerned, the real hero of the Portland spy ring was Lonsdale (otherwise Molodi), sentenced to five years, but released to the Soviets in exchange for Greville Wynne, an Englishman accused of spying in Soviet Russia who had deliberately been held in harsh conditions to speed the exchange. As for the Krogers, they both received 20-year sentences. Their exchange in 1969 for Gerald Brooke, a young British university lecturer, revealed further evidence,

Donald Maclean, seen here in June 1951, perched on the desk of Sir John Balfour, at the British Embassy in Washington. Maclean served as First Secretary, but was later revealed as a KGB agent.

if it was needed, of the cynical ruthlessness of the KGB. Four years earlier, Brooke, guilty of naiveté rather than calculated espionage, had smuggled pamphlets into the Soviet Union attacking the Communist regime. These were the work of one of the many West German-based Russian émigré organizations, some covertly funded by the CIA. As might have been anticipated, it had been penetrated by the KGB, and Brooke was now arrested for peddling 'subversive' literature and confined to the camps. It was made clear to the West that Brooke would continue to be held until a suitable exchange for one or more of their own spies could be arranged. The Soviets went further. Stories were planted in the media that Brooke's health was deteriorating and that he could die if he was not released. The deal, made in 1969, by the British government was the exchange of Brooke for the Krogers. This brought about a furious clash with the security services, who now perceived that the Soviets held all the cards: no Briton travelling behind the Iron Curtain could count on safety while Britain held a spy whom the Soviets wanted back. The KGB now possessed a major advantage.

GEORGE BLAKE

The late 1940s and early 1950s were years that revealed just how badly British intelligence had been penetrated by the KGB. Most shocking was the recall of Kim Philby from Washington, where he had been the SIS representative with the duty of liaising with the CIA. This had been a billet that had given him limitless access to top-secret papers, much of whose contents were passed to his Moscow bosses. At the same time, Britain's spymasters closed in on two more KGB agents, Donald Maclean (1913–83), head of the American Department at the Foreign Office, and Guy Burgess (1911–63), who had also served in Washington. The date that they were due to be interviewed was leaked to them by another traitor, Anthony Blunt (1907–83), and the two defected to Moscow in May 1951.

No time was lost in recruiting a successor to the discredited Philby. This was another SIS officer, 29-year-old George Blake (b. 1922), son of an Egyptian-born Jewish trader and naturalized Briton named Albert Behar. His Dutch mother had been widowed in 1936. George had been living in Rotterdam when the Germans invaded. He served in the Dutch resistance, later fleeing from the Gestapo along an SOE escape line, and eventually reaching Britain. He next joined the Royal Navy, where he secured a job in naval intelligence in Hamburg, following the Allied occupation of Germany. His skill in languages attracted the attention of the Foreign Office in London, which posted him to the Far Eastern department. In 1949, he went to South Korea as vice consul in Seoul. A year later, following the outbreak of the Korean War, he was interned by the North Koreans and sent to a POW camp in Manchuria.

CAPTURED

Intent on securing his future at the end of the war, Blake handed his Communist captors a note in Russian addressed to the nearest embassy,

On the direction of his Soviet controller, and with the further aid of fellow spy Anthony Blunt, Guy Burgess was assigned to warn his fellow agent Donald Maclean that British counterintelligence was closing in. At the very last moment, Burgess, notoriously impulsive and unpredictable, defected with Maclean.

INDIA AND THE KGB

In searching for promising outlets in the developing world, the KGB devoted most of its energy to India, which Stalin had dismissed with contempt as an imperialist puppet. Mahatma Gandhi, who had led India to independence, was dismissed in the *Great Soviet Encyclopaedia* as a reactionary 'who …betrayed the people and helped the imperialists against them; aped the ascetics; pretended in a demagogic way to be a supporter of India independence and an enemy of the British, and widely exploited religious prejudice'. In their book on the KGB, Christopher Andrew and Oleg Gordievsky state that the campaign of vilification went back as far as the days of the British Raj, when the Indian Communist Party was receiving instructions from Moscow and its messages were being accepted by the Intelligence Branch (IB) based in New Delhi. Until the early 1950s, Moscow stressed the necessity and importance of overthrowing 'the reactionary government of Jawaharlal Nehru'.

Oleg Kalugin, once the youngest General in the KGB responsible for monitoring its activities abroad, maintained: 'We had scores of sources through the Indian government – in intelligence, counter-intelligence, the defence and foreign ministries and the police.'

According to the high security KGB files brought to the West by Vasily Mitrokhin, Soviet intelligence set out deliberately to exploit corruption within the regime of Mrs Indira Gandhi, who received suitcases stuffed with bank notes to finance her wing of the Congress Party. It is believed that Mrs Gandhi was unaware that some of the suitcases replenishing Congress's coffers came from Moscow via the KGB. However, the same cannot be said of Lalit Narayan Mishra, her principal fundraiser, described in the second volume of *The Mitrokin Archive* as 'looking the part of the corrupt politician he increasingly became'.

The charm offensive on India was stepped up, particularly after Indira Gandhi in 1971 signed a Treaty of Peace, Friendship and Co-operation with the Soviet Union. Restrictions were lifted on the number of Soviet diplomats and trade officials able to operate in India. The benefit to the KGB was obvious: life became easier for agents working under cover. Furthermore, the extent of Soviet influence strengthened. By 1973, the KGB had on its payroll ten Indian newspapers as well as a press agency. In the previous year, it was claimed that some 3700 articles had been planted in the press.

But the KGB grew overconfident, paying insufficient attention to events inside the country and failing to anticipate the backlash against Mrs Gandhi, which followed accusations of fraud in the elections of 1972, for which she was convicted. Determined but inflexible, her response was to introduce a state of emergency and imprison political opponents. In 1977, she lost power, but the next year returned under the banner of her own party, the Congress (I) (I for Indira). Her attempts to resolve political problems in the state of Punjab led to a crackdown on the Sikh secessionist movement and an attack upon the Golden Temple, the holiest of Sikh shrines. On 31 October 1984 came retaliation, when Indira Gandhi was shot dead by two Sikh guards in the garden of her house. The KGB now blamed the assassination on the CIA.

Mrs Gandhi's elder son, Rajiv, succeeded her, visiting Moscow in March 1985 to forge what he hoped would be close links with President Mikhail Gorbachev. But the response was lukewarm. The Cold War was coming to an end, lessening the usefulness of India for KGB active measures, and Russia now had problems of her own. The Indo-Soviet special relationship, to which the KGB had devoted so much energy, withered and died, while the KGB itself had just six years to run.

requesting a contact to whom he could pass on important information. Eventually identifying himself to a KGB interviewer, he volunteered to work as a Soviet agent. Codenamed DIOMID, he was assigned Sergei Alexsandrovich Konradshev as his controller. Back in England, he went into the field as an SIS officer and was despatched to Berlin, one of the most sensitive posts of the Cold War. A major advantage for Blake was his close contact with Reinhard Gehlen, which meant he was ideally placed to spy on West German intelligence, above all to learn about the so-called Stopwatch/Gold operation. Masterminded by the CIA and SIS, this was a plan to dig a clandestine tunnel across the sector border from West to East Berlin to intercept land lines running from the Soviet military and intelligence headquarters in Karlshorst. Blake's first act was to forward to his controller a carbon copy of the minutes of an SIS–CIA conference on the project.

The follow-up was swift. Markus Wolf, woken at dawn by the Minister for State Security, Ernst Wollweber, was driven to meet a party of diggers from a special department of the Red Army. At the tunnel site, they used blowtorches to cut through steel and penetrated an underground chamber, which contained bundles of cables, each of which had an amplifier attached. Here signals were picked up, magnified and diverted along cables disappearing through a trap door in the floor. A shaft led to a steel-lined tunnel disappearing in the direction of the American radar station. The cables being tapped were those carrying some of the Red Army's most secret communications, and the intercepts had provided the latest information on the improved nuclear capability of the Soviet air force in East Germany, its new bomber fleet and twin-jet radar interceptors, as well as installations and personnel of the Soviet atomic energy programme. All this amounted to a remarkable intelligence coup.

'IMPERIAL AGGRESSION'

Naturally enough, the Soviets lost no time in denouncing it. Colonel Ivan Kotsiuba, East Berlin's Soviet media chief, was more than willing to conduct tours of the tunnel for Western reporters and photographers, while working himself up into a lather of indignation at intolerable 'imperial aggression' and 'international gangsterism'. At the same time American papers, such as

George Blake, the unrepentant double agent, had links with Communism originating when he was a teenager in Cairo and came under the influence of the Egyptian Communist party. In England, he served both British intelligence and the KGB, where it was reckoned he betrayed around 40 Allied agents to the Soviets.

Artefacts of a spy: the contents of Kim Philby's Moscow apartment were released by the Soviets following his death and were auctioned by Sothebys in London in July 1994.

the *Washington Post,* hailed 'Yankee resourcefulness and ingenuity'. As yet, it had not proved possible for the British and Americans to finger George Blake as the mole involved. The evidence was not quite sufficient, even though one of the messages intercepted revealed the existence of a British Soviet agent working in Berlin.

Then in January 1961 came the defection to Berlin of Lieutenant Colonel Michael Goleniewski, former deputy head of Polish counter-intelligence. Debriefed, he revealed George Blake's identity. At his trial, held *in camera,*

Blake was sentenced to 42 years imprisonment, said to be one year for every agent he had betrayed to Moscow. In fact, after serving just six years, he managed to break out of Wormwood Scrubs, after plans made with an Irish criminal named Sean Bourke, who later swore that he had no connection whatever with politics or the KGB. Whether this was engineered by the Soviets in a bid to look after its own has remained a mystery.

THE ASSASSINATION OF GEORGI MARKOV

It was in September 1978 that the power of the KGB was demonstrated on the streets of London. A prominent Bulgarian dissident intellectual, Georgi Markov, was assassinated, not by a bullet from the barrel of a gun but by a minuscule pellet. Markov, well-known in his own country for his plays and books, had defected to Britain, where he went to work for the BBC World Service, Radio Free Europe and the German *Deutsche Welle*. He became steadily more outspoken in his criticism of Bulgaria's Communist Party. Its leader was Todor Zhivkov, a Stalinist hardliner whose control had become as near absolute as was possible for a Moscow satellite.

> Bulgaria's Communist party was a Moscow satellite exercising near total control.

How all this came to affect events in London has been detailed by Brian Freemantle, who interviewed Annabel Markov, Georgi's widow, for his 1982 book *KGB*. The couple were living in the south London suburb of Clapham with their daughter Sasha, and received a warning, from a source which has remained unidentified, that Markov was a target for assassination. He was warned that he should be careful to eat and drink only with close friends. The Markovs took the precaution of having their telephone number made ex-directory and were wary of any new faces among Bulgarian émigré groups. As far as they could determine, there were none; nonetheless Markov was closely shadowed. On Thursday 7 September 1978, he was on a 12-hour tour of duty at Bush House, the headquarters of the BBC World Service situated in the Strand area of London.

STABBED

He followed his usual routine by driving his green and cream Simca van from his home. Because parking restrictions prevented parking nearer to Bush House, his habit was to leave the vehicle on the south side of the Thames and walk the rest of the way. At 6.30 p.m., after reading the evening news, he would leave Bush House, walk across the Waterloo Bridge and bring the Simca closer to the BBC building, where parking by that time was permitted. In the course of his walk, he passed a queue near the National Theatre. Suddenly he felt a sharp thrust against his right thigh, followed by a brief, burning pain. Twisting instinctively, Markov caused a man facing him

A replica of the umbrella used by the KGB agent to kill Georgi Markov, on display at the International Spy Museum in Washington, D.C. The Communist regime in Bulgaria had a particularly ugly record for murdering those who opposed the regime, and it is unlikely that these assassinations lacked the approval of the Soviets. The pinhead platinum pellet containing the ricin poison was the handiwork of the KGB Technical Operations Directorate. The slow-working poison leads to cardiovascular collapse. An unsuspecting doctor could easily diagnose death through heart attack, a fact which suggests other killings may have gone undetected.

to drop his umbrella, then retrieve it with an apology in heavily accented English. The man, later described as thick set and about 40 years old, then departed rapidly aboard a hastily summoned taxi.

It was past 7 p.m. when Markov arrived back in the office, told a colleague what had happened and showed him a small red mark on his thigh resembling a harmless insect bite. Back home at around 10.30 p.m., he went to sleep on a bed set up in his study so that he need not disturb his wife when he got up for the dawn shift back to Bush House. But at 2 a.m. she heard him moving around, and discovered that he had vomited and had a temperature of 40° Centigrade (104° Fahrenheit). He was removed to hospital, where his rapid deterioration and abnormally high fever led him to intensive care. In lucid moments, he recounted his experience on Waterloo Bridge.

An X-ray of the red puncture mark showed an object of high metallic density. Following Markov's death on Monday 11 September, this was revealed to be a tiny metal ball, certainly small enough to have fitted into the tip of an umbrella. This ball, together with tissue samples, was rushed for analysis to the British Government's Chemical Defence establishment at Porton Down in Wiltshire. There, scientists found that the ball contained lethal ricin, one of the world's most powerful toxins, a single grain of which can kill an estimated 30,000 people. Markov's inquest returned a verdict that he had been 'killed unlawfully'.

KGB IMPLICATED

The connection of the killing with Bulgaria seemed virtually certain and with it the link to the Soviet Union, which at that time was the major producer of the metal used for the ricin pellet. As the Mitrokhin documents were to reveal, Markov's broadcasts had come to the attention of the *Durzhavna Sigurnost* (DS), the Bulgarian secret police, which worked closely with the KGB and specialized in political assassination. The Bulgarian leader

Zhivkov, infuriated by Georgi Markov's hostile broadcasts from London, complained to Moscow, demanding action. At first, Andropov and his advisers were reluctant to become involved in any proposed elimination of Markov. Eventually, however, they agreed to provide the means but made it clear there was to be no direct participation by Moscow. On that basis, the DS went ahead.

In charge of the operation was Sergei Mikhailovich Golubev, head of the Foreign Intelligence Directorate of the KGB, and a poisons expert. He worked with Oleg Kalugin, a senior colleague who had direct access to the Directorate's top secret poisons laboratory. One of his first tasks was to contact his agents in Washington and instruct them to obtain a number of umbrellas – the deliberate choice of American ones was, of course, to conceal any connection with either Moscow or Sofia. The tip of the chosen umbrella became a gun, firing the pellet that killed Markov.

'THE TRAMP'

As to the actual assassin, the Bulgarian daily newspaper *Dnevnik* carried a serialization in June 2005 of secret service files, and named the man believed to be Markov's killer. The article was the work of Hristo Hristov, an investigative journalist based in Sofia, who had researched the case for six years.

He now came up with the name of Francesco Giullino, a Dane of Italian origin, who posed as an antiques salesman and the owner of a picture-framing business, travelling Europe in an Austrian-registered caravan. He was recruited as an agent in 1970 after being caught smuggling drugs and currency. Codenamed 'Agent Piccadilly', Giullino made three reconnaissance trips to London to prepare for the killing of Markov, who had been codenamed 'Skitnik' ('Tramp').

He flew from London to Italy the day after the attack. The DS files that were consulted by Hristo Hristov are genuine, according to Rumen Danov, special adviser for national security to Sheelu Zhelev, Bulgaria's first post-Communist president. Additionally, Oleg Kalugin, the former head of K Directorate (Counter Intelligence) confirmed that the KGB was responsible for Markov's killing.

Following the collapse of the Bulgarian Communist regime in 1989, the Bulgarian authorities admitted their role in killing Georgi Markov (above). In late 1992, General Vladimir Todorov, the former Bulgarian intelligence chief, received a prison sentence for destroying ten volumes of relevant material.

ANTHONY BLUNT

In 1979, one year after Georgi Markov's death, international interest again focused on Britain, this time to the public disgrace of a parson's son who seemed, on the surface at least, quintessentially English, in terms of class, education and manners. Peter Wright from MI5 considered Sir Anthony Blunt to be 'one of the most elegant, charming and cultivated men I have met. He could speak five languages, and the range and depth of his knowledge was profoundly impressive'. But as Wright went on to make clear, 'Blunt was capable of slipping from art historian and scholar one minute, to intelligence bureaucrat the next, to spy, to waspish homosexual, to languid establishmentarian'.

> 'Blunt…held a position of trust which was turning him into a creature of the noblest, oldest and most sensitive branch of the Establishment: the Crown itself.'
>
> —Andrew Boyle,
> *The Climate of Treason*

Matters were brought to a head with the publication in 1979 of *The Climate of Treason* by the writer Andrew Boyle. Because no formal charges had ever been made against Blunt, a distinguished art historian who had been knighted by the Queen, and because of the restrictions of Britain's libel laws, he was referred to in Boyle's book as 'Maurice'. To those who had followed his career, and particularly to those who had known his fellow spies Burgess, Maclean and Philby, it was possible to interpret certain clues left by Boyle. Outsiders were none the wiser. Thus when in November 1979, a member of the House of Commons, Ted Leadbitter, asked in Parliament whether the Prime Minister would make a statement on the actions 'of an individual … in relation to the security of the United Kingdom', it came as considerable surprise when Mrs Margaret Thatcher replied: 'The name … is that of Sir Anthony Blunt'.

TALENT SPOTTER

Back in 1964, Arthur Martin, an MI5 officer, had called on Blunt at his London apartment with direct evidence that he had worked for the Soviets. While a young don at Trinity College Cambridge, Blunt had been recruited as a Soviet agent, assigned the task of talent-spotting other possible adherents. It was later claimed that he also blackmailed fellow homosexuals into becoming spies. At the outbreak of war in 1939, Blunt took a commission in the British army and served briefly in an army field intelligence unit with the British Expeditionary Force, enabling him to pass on lists of operators which proved of use in the upcoming Cold War. On his return home he was recruited by MI5, serving in a section among many European exile groups, details of whom reached his Soviet controller. Ostensibly, Blunt's spying ended in 1945, when he left MI5 to pursue an academic and artistic career that included the post of Surveyor of the Queen's Pictures, which included cataloguing the Royal art treasures at Windsor Castle. This did not deter the investigations of the British security services, which knew that Blunt had been seen in the company of Burgess and Maclean before their disappearance. A series of interviews, including hours of taped interrogations, failed to shake him. Then in January 1964, Michael Witney Straight, an American who had studied at Trinity and who had admitted his Communist past to the FBI, claimed that Blunt had tried to recruit him as a Soviet spy.

Additionally, a released KGB file revealed that during the war Leo Long, another graduate from the Cambridge nursery of spies who had gone on to

Anthony Blunt claimed that he became a Soviet spy not for ideological reasons but because he believed that Soviet Russia was the only force capable of defeating Nazi Germany in World War II. However British Prime Minister Margaret Thatcher declared: 'There is no doubt that British interests were severely damaged by his activities.' After his exposure, Blunt faced TV cameras maintaining: 'I did not betray my conscience'.

Cuba's Fidel Castro (second from left), seen here viewing the Moscow May Day procession on 1 May 1963. He is flanked by Marshal Rodion Malinovsky (left), the Soviet Premier Nikita Khruschev (right) and the latter's successor, Leonid Brezhnev.

work at the War Office, was an NKVD/NKGB agent. He had been run by Blunt, with whom he held weekly meetings. Long passed on pieces of information he felt were likely to be of use to the Soviets. These included reports of troop movements with comments by British intelligence on the progress of the war. Much of these reports were derived from decrypts made at Bletchley Park, which housed the Government Code and Cypher School. With the coming of peace, Blunt pressed Long to renew his spying activities. Nor was this the sole espionage activity at this time. Decrypts of communications between Moscow and the Soviet Embassy in London revealed that a third agent, codenamed Baron, had been working on Bletchley Park's intercepts. His identity remains unknown.

CONFESSION

Those who questioned Blunt further in 1964, citing the revelations of Michael Straight, held out an added inducement to come clean: he would be immune from prosecution in return for confession and information on his activities and contacts. He eventually agreed. The arrangement, which deeply

THE KGB IN CUBA

When it came to operating highly sophisticated electronic espionage, the KGB remained active until the collapse of the Soviet Union. It operated an unrivalled worldwide signals intelligence network (SIGINT) from its headquarters at the main KGB building in Moscow's Dzerzhinsky Square. Overall control lay with the Sixteenth (SIGINT) Directive, formed in the 1960s and with Soviet diplomatic missions in more than 60 countries. By the end of the 1970s, the number of Sixteenth Directorate employees reached 2000. The task of the Sixteenth Directorate was to intercept and decrypt material from foreign embassies and missions, and also to detect their communications equipment. The result, in the words of President Reagan in 1983, was a network was 'the largest of its kind in the world' with 'acres and acres of...intelligence monitors'.

When it came to targeting the United States, the SIGINT facility established at Lourdes in Cuba was reckoned by US intelligence to be among the most powerful. Situated less than a thousand miles from Key West, Florida, it was operated by the Cuban secret services, the GRU Soviet security and the Federal Agency for Government Communications and Information (FAPSI), the Soviet counterpart of the US National Security Agency. Codenamed 'Termite-P', its equipment intercepted communications that were transmitted by British satellites. Equipment for the time was state-of-the-art: a fixed 12 metre (40 ft) stationary dish antenna and a mobile 7 metre (23 ft) dish antenna mounted on a covered lorry. This facilitated the interception of microwave communications 'downlinked' from US satellites. Over time, the Cuban complex became capable of monitoring government communications throughout the southeastern US and between the US and Europe.

Details of these activities, and much else in Cuba came from Stanislav Lunev, former colonel in the GRU. He declared in a press interview: 'Lourdes receives and collects intercepts by spy satellites ships and planes in the Atlantic region, making it a fully fledged regional command and control centre. Its targets include the interception of sensitive diplomatic, commercial and economic traffic and even private US communications.'

On 16 October 2001 Moscow suddenly notified Havana of its intention to shut down the signals intelligence centre in Lourdes, followed by confirmation the next day by President Putin at a meeting at the Russian Federation Ministry of Defence.

In the West, the reason was considered to be predominantly economic. The annual payment to Cuba for the centre was $200 million (6 billion roubles), the total cost during its final 10 years being $3 billion. On 22 September 2003, Defence Minister Ivanov declared that the dismantling of the military bases was complete.

Sceptics point out that as late as the summer of 1999, the US FBI and State Department discovered a very elaborate Russian listening device planted in the heart of the US State Department. It was being operated at a remote distance by a Russian spy in the United States under diplomatic cover. Additionally, in the same year the *Washington Times* of 26 July was reporting that the US Ambassador to Russia, James Colleens, had been instructed to warn senior Russian officials to reduce the substantial number of Russian intelligence officers operating in the United States.

Steven Aftergood of the Federation of American Scientists, a Washington-based study group that monitored developments over the following three years, has confirmed: 'It appears the facility was indeed shut down'. Nevertheless, his group are watching closely how the reorganization of surveillance activities will affect the security services of the Russian Federation.

Vladimir Semichastny (left), Chairman of the KGB and one of its arch intriguers, is seen here in 1964, the year he was involved in ousting Nikita Khruschev from the Soviet leadership at Leonid Brezhnev's instigation. Here, he is sitting with Rudolf Abel (second from left), former director of the Soviet spy network on the United States and Konon Molody (second from right), better known in the West as Gordon Lonsdale, central figure in the Portland Ring.

disgusted many of those who came to know of Blunt's guilt, was admitted by Margaret Thatcher's statement in the House of Commons: 'The Queen's Private Secretary was informed both of Blunt's confession and of the immunity from prosecution … Blunt was not required to resign his appointment in the Royal Household, which was unpaid. It carried with it no access to classified information and no risk to security and the security authorities thought it desirable not to put at risk his co-operation'. Following the publication of *The Climate of Treason*, Blunt was stripped of his title. If this was meant to be sufficient to end the affair and bring an end to the various scandals, Witney Straight forcibly disagreed, claiming there was still a KGB spy working at the very heart of MI5. No name was ever revealed.

As for Philby, who had arrived in Moscow via Beirut in July 1963, his political views did not appear to have changed. In his book *My Silent War*, published in 1979, he wrote: 'There is still an awful lot of work ahead; there will be ups and downs … But as I look over Moscow from my study window, I can see the solid foundations of the future I glimpsed at Cambridge.'

THE BREZHNEV ERA

But the foundations were anything but solid, and had been crumbling for decades, particularly in Eastern Europe. By 1956, Poland stood on the brink of rebellion; card-carrying Communists and fellow travellers were defecting at an alarming rate. Premier Nikita Khrushchev presented the Soviet Union, burdened with a sick economy, with a fresh party programme. This urged deep reforms in industry, agriculture and party organization. The result only inflamed wide antagonism, including among KGB leaders who feared their power being undermined. In the autumn of 1964, Khrushchev left for a holiday in the Black Sea, seen off by smiling colleagues. But these were smilers with knives.

On 13 October, he was summoned back to Moscow for an urgent meeting of the Praesidium. There was no welcome back at the airport. The only greeting came from Vladimir Yefimovich Semichastny, head of the KGB. In case Khrushchev had been determined to show opposition to his dismissal, a dossier had been assembled by the KGB outlining his role in the Stalinist purges. Khrushchev went quietly, offered a pension and agreeable fringe benefits. His 'resignation' was officially due to 'advanced age' and 'ill-health'. When he died six years later, *Pravda* noted briefly the passing of 'N S Khrushchev, a pensioner'.

The fact that Leonid Brezhnev (1906–82) succeeded Khrushchev hardly came as a surprise. As chairman of the Praesidium of the Supreme Soviet in 1960, he had resigned four years later to become Khrushchev's direct assistant as second secretary of the Central Committee, achieving full membership of the *Politburo*. But he had not been after a cosy partnership

ANDREI SAKHAROV

There were strict limits to the professed 'liberalism' of the Brezhnev era: the KGB remained as powerful as ever. One campaign launched to discredit dissidents focused on the physicist and human rights activist Andrei Sakharov. In October 1975, he was awarded the Nobel Peace Prize, the judges stating that 'Sakharov's fearless personal commitment in upholding the fundamental principles for peace between men is a powerful inspiration'.

Mitrokhin revealed that Yuri Andropov, then Chairman of the KGB, approved a document entitled 'Complex Operational Measures to Expose the Political Background to the Award of the Nobel Peace Prize to Sakharov'. The KGB's Foreign Intelligence Directorate received instructions 'to inspire articles and speeches by public and political personalities ... to develop the theme that the award of the Nobel Peace Prize to Sakharov was an attempt by certain political circles to slow down the process of détente ...' Additionally, letters of protest were received by the Nobel Committee of the Norwegian parliament and by the media throughout Western Europe. Andropov failed to prevent the bestowal of the award to Sakharov and had to be content with a minor consolation: the award-winner was forbidden to travel outside the Soviet Union to collect it.

It was by no means the last of Sakharov's clashes with Andropov, who made sure that the dissident was exiled to the city of Gorky (Nizhny Novgorod), which became closed to outsiders. His offence had been to protest against the Soviet invasion of Afghanistan in 1979.

As the short-lived Soviet General Secretary – he held the office for just 16 months before his death – Andropov was regarded by many as a ruthless intriguer and power seeker. Other commentators saw him as a cautious but relatively humane reformer and innovator.

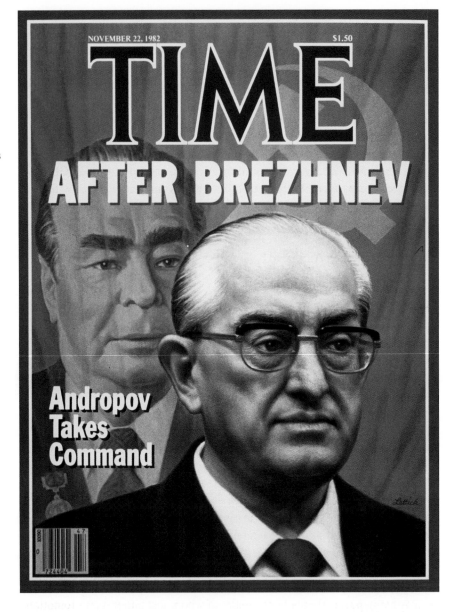

NOVEMBER 22, 1982 $1.50

TIME

AFTER BREZHNEV

Andropov Takes Command

with anyone: he had been seeking Khrushchev's job and its attendant power. On the surface, Brezhnev's rule seemed to foreshadow some of the reforms that were to lead to the collapse of the Soviet Union. Personal dictatorship gradually gave way to oligarchy, collective rule by a privileged minority, the birth of a new class born to a hitherto classless society. Furthermore, the 1970s saw a period of *detente*, or peaceful co-existence in US-Soviet relations. Authority was relaxed and some political issues were more open to debate; religious belief and practice were cautiously revived.

The developing world was regarded by the Soviets as an essential area to score its major successes in the Cold War. Andropov made clear his intentions in an official Minute. 'We must be the first to establish contacts with important individuals in those countries where we do not have embassies, and to send our officers there on short or long-term visits.' In Afghanistan, after Soviet military intervention in 1979, the KGB unleashed a regime that rivalled the worst horrors of the Stalin era, the aim being to combat 'ideological sabotage' and help stem 'the overthrow of socialism'. On the evening of 27 December 1979, acting on *Politburo* authority, Soviet troops flew into Afghanistan, headed by an assault group of crack KGB commandos, dressed in Afghan uniforms and travelling in vehicles with Afghan markings (see page 178). On the way to the presidential palace, the commandos machine-gunned guards after being stopped at a military checkpoint. They then forced their way into the palace, gunning down President Hafizullah Amin and his mistress. For the moment at least, thuggery seemed the most effective tool the KGB possessed.

THE COLLAPSE OF THE SOVIET UNION

By the early 1980s, Brezhnev was reaching the end of what had proved to be a long physical and mental decline. With his death in 1982, the Soviet Union had less than 10 years of life remaining. But for 70-year-old Andropov, who became the first KGB chief to be elected Party leader by the *Politburo,* and his successor 72-year-old Konstantin Chernenko (1911–85), the fates were little better. The two men died within a year of one another.

The first leader of the Soviet Union born after the Russian Revolution was Mikhail Gorbachev (b. 1931). From a peasant family, he had risen rapidly, becoming a member of the Communist Party's Central Committee by his mid-30s. In March 1985, he was elected General Secretary. Those who were charmed by his air of seeming affability soon learned the danger of underestimating him. He lived up to Gromyko's widely quoted description as the man with 'a nice smile and steel teeth'. Right from the start, Gorbachev was keen to make his mark, instituting personnel changes in both Party and government, which were encapsulated by the terms *glasnost* ('openness') and *perestroika* ('restructuring'). Those who had been Brezhnev's cronies were seen as being political opponents, many of whom lost either their promotion prospects or their jobs.

Priority was given to enhancing the immense resources of the KGB, by that time a 400,000-strong security and intelligence empire inside the Soviet Union alone, bolstered by 200,000 border troops and a sprawling network of informers. Its foreign intelligence arm, the First Chief Directorate (FCD), underwent the most significant growth: from about 3000 personnel in the mid-1960s to 12,000 in the mid-1980s. Training of officers centred at the FCD's Andropov Institute was vigorous. In charge was a commandant with

AFGHANISTAN

Backed by the entire *Politburo,* the KGB on the evening of 27 December 1979 unleashed a wholesale assault on Afghanistan that rivalled even the worst excesses of the Stalin era. The aim was to combat 'ideological sabotage' and a bid 'to overthrow socialism'. Its origins lay in the aftermath of World War II, when the United Nations had the task of putting a brake on Soviet expansion. Both the US and the Soviet Union courted the Afghans via economic aid and development, the Soviets emerging the successful suitors with their support of Afghanistan's communist People's Democratic Party (PDPA). At the time of the assault, the Afghan government was led by Hafizullah Amin, who faced intense opposition. The striving for Marxist-Leninist reforms clashed with the Afghan mullahs and loosely aligned *mujahedin* groups, who declared a *jihad* against the pro-Soviet regime.

At the start of the invasion, the fleets of Soviet Antonov transport aircraft at Kabul International Airport disgorged scores of troops backed by a formidable array of tanks and trucks. The day belonged to elite commandos of the Alpha Anti Terrorist squad of the KGB, led by Colonel Grigori Boyarinov of Department 8 (Special Operations). Their preparation had been typically meticulous: they were dressed not as Russians but in Afghan uniforms and they travelled in Afghan-marked military vehicles. Resistance was fierce: more than a hundred KGB were killed along with Boyarinov. Once in the presidential palace, the invaders opened fire, gunning down Hafizullah Amin.

The radio station, airport and other key locations were seized, while four motorized infantry and armoured divisions had crossed the Afghan–Soviet border. Within hours, the entire city was under Soviet control. Amin was replaced by a Soviet puppet, Babrak Karmal.

As would have been expected, the KGB lost no time in forming the local secret police, naming it

Khedamate-e Etelea'at-E Dawlati (State Information Agency – KHAD). It was headed by Muhammad Najibullah, described in *The Mitrokhin Archive* as, 'A man capable of intimidating opponents by his mere physical presence'. Amnesty International assembled evidence of widespread and systematic torture of men, women and children. Najibullah sometimes executed prisoners himself. His preferred methods, according to survivors of his prisoners, was to beat his victims to the ground, then kick them to death. Near famine conditions were reported in many provinces, and infant mortality from malnutrition reached 85 per cent in some areas. Tortures and executions followed a familiar pattern. In the Poli Charki concentration camp, some six miles from Kabul, it was estimated that some 30,000 had perished by the early 1980s.

For its part, the American CIA went on to launch extensive and sophisticated covert operations, including supplying armoury and spy satellite images to assist the *mujahedin.* CIA-trained resistance fighters conducted bombings and ambushed Soviet leaders in Kabul. Faced with all this, Mikhail Gorbachev ousted Karmal from office and into retirement in 1986, replacing him with the infinitely more ruthless Najibullah. But the Soviets were facing defeat. A succession of heavy raids by the *mujahedin* forced them eventually to abandon Kandahar airfield. By 1986 the Reagan administration was supplying Stinger air-to-surface missiles to the Afghan resistance.

The Soviets hung on in Afghanistan until 1989, withdrawing after ten years of an aggressive American policy and defiant *mujahedin* fighters. By then, the United Nations High Commissioner for Refugees (UNHCR) estimated that one million Afghans had died in the fighting between Soviet troops and the *mujahedin* resistance forces. Muhammad Najibullah was seized by the Taliban and executed, his body hung from a lamp post.

the rank of general, who was responsible for agent recruitment and courses that included instructing agents in such disciplines as successful surveillance and arranging covert contacts. But being a KGB member entailed a great deal more: it took over just about every aspect of an agent's life. Marriage for men was made compulsory; wives were expected to be more than dutiful spouses, but also partners in intelligence.

GLASNOST

Gorbachev instigated reforms at such a speed that by early 1987 he considered he was strong enough to risk antagonism from established institutions, the KGB included. It was not long before there were signs of opposition, particularly from *Politburo* traditionalists who saw a threat to their long-established empires. One of these, Egor Ligachev, the second-ranking Politburo member, declared that those at the top of the KGB would

Mikhail Gorbachev (left) and Boris Yeltsin (centre) talk in the wake of the attempted 1991 coup. By 25 December, Gorbachev had resigned as Soviet president and the red hammer and sickle flag of the Soviet Union had been lowered from the Kremlin, replaced with the tricolour of the Russian state.

not tolerate reforms that went too far. He declared in a strident speech: 'There must be a clear awareness that the restructuring is taking place in our state and society under the leadership of the Communist Party, within the framework of socialism and in the interests of socialism. This revolutionary process will be reliably protected against subversive intrigues.'

Internal opposition was not the only challenge facing Gorbachev and the KGB. The published revelations of Stalin's brutalities began to spread to Soviet satellites. Prominent among these was East Germany with its enormously repressive *Stasi,* which had proved a good pupil of the KGB. The same methods were there: controlled media, a vast network of informants to repress subversives, the encouragement of family members to spy on one another through physical threats and the fear of blackmail. Before Gorbachev, the *Stasi* had a force of more than 90,000 uniformed and plain-clothed agents with around 175,000 officials on its books – roughly one for every hundred individuals.

> Gorbachev intended to downgrade the KGB into a looser framework with power and authority going to the republics.

But its days were numbered. The most far-reaching of Gorbachev's foreign reforms was to allow Eastern Bloc nations to determine their own internal affairs, leading to what was effectively the ending of the Cold War. Calls for greater independence from Moscow's rule became more shrill, led by the Baltic republics annexed by Stalin in 1940. Like a burning fuse, demand spread to the Soviet republics of Georgia, Ukraine, Armenia and Azerbaijan. A time bomb was ticking; the spectre of a putsch loomed. In a speech made in parliament on 17 June 1991, the KGB Chairman Vladimir Kryuchkov raised the temperature still further, citing Gorbachev's contacts with the West as proof that he intended to destroy the Soviet Union. He claimed to possess proof of the conspiracy and alleged that an American mole was installed in the Kremlin. To powerful conservative elements, all this was intolerable; there could be no question of coming to terms with the inevitable demise of the Soviet Union. Seemingly, Gorbachev was fully intending to downgrade the KGB into a much looser framework, transferring much of the power and authority to the republics.

PUTSCH

If he scented a putsch, Gorbachev gave no sign, leaving as planned with his wife Raisa on a vacation to his dacha on the island of Forus in the Crimea. The leaders of the coup, who included Kryuchkov, formed an eight-man National Emergency Committee, announcing that Gorbachev had been removed from his position as president through illness. For three days, the couple were kept under house arrest. But a firm stand against the coup was made by Boris Yeltsin (b. 1931), a radical reformist and ambitious rival to

Gorbachev, who had been elected Chairman of the Supreme Soviet of the Russian Socialist Republic the previous May. He believed in a rapid transition by Russia to a market economy, even if that meant the disintegration of the Soviet Union and the end of Communism. Fatally overestimating public support, the military deployed to the Russian Parliament, but found it surrounded by both armed and unarmed civilians. There, the soldiers were treated to a memorable harangue from Yeltsin from on top of a tank.

The coup collapsed. Gorbachev and his wife were released, but Gorbachev had lost the initiative and power swung in the direction of Boris Yeltsin. The final eclipse of the Soviet Union came on 24 December 1991, with the Russian Federation taking the Soviet Union's seat in the United Nations. The next day, President Gorbachev resigned; the Union of Soviet Socialist Republics ceased to exist along with the KGB, which was restructured as the FSB (*Federalnaya Sluzhba Bezopasnosti* – Russian Security and Intelligence Service). The rest of Yeltsin's term as President saw

In Moscow on 26 October 2002 Vladimir Putin (right) and Interior Minister Boris Gryzlov (left) are in formal stance while Nikolai Patrushev (centre) is today's impassive face of Russian security: the chief of the FSB.

a series of economic crises for Russia: skyrocketing prices, vicious cuts in government spending and heavy new taxes heralding a protracted depression. In addition, Yeltsin's health went into severe decline, exacerbated by his alcoholism. His approval ratings plummeted to 5 per cent in his last months in office; he resigned on 31 December 1999.

THE PRESENT

In accordance with the Russian constitution, Prime Minister Vladimir Putin (b. 1952) became an acting President until new elections the following year. On 26 March 2000 he was elected President of the Russian Federation. As the only former chief of the KGB to hold the position, he proceeded to surround himself with more former intelligence officers than any of his predecessors.

Early on, there were moves to give the FSB a more human face. The use of rhetoric from the Stalin era, calling for the onward march of world revolution, was quietly soft-pedalled. The emphasis switched to the defence of traditional Russian values and 'defence of the cultural, spiritual and moral inheritance'.

Russia had long fostered an intelligence elite and there were those who had no intention of relinquishing their position. From its early days, the FSB has convened a series of annual history seminars, held under the auspices of the Andropov Institute, which members of the FSB are encouraged to attend. Both resident historians and academics have given presentations on Russian links with police and intelligence organizations going back to the days of the *Okhrana,* OGPU, MVD and NKVD.

As for traditional spying, the British newspaper *The Independent*, citing government sources, reported in October 2004 that Russia had resumed Cold War levels of spying, with at least 32 of its diplomats seeking information about the United Kingdom's military, technical and political strengths and capabilities. Alex Standish, Editor of the influential *Jane's Intelligence Digest,* stated that: 'Putin is rapidly building up intelligence systems that have been allowed to fall into decline under the Yeltsin era.' The conclusion of the second volume of *The Mitrokhin Archive* points to the existence of a multi-volume history, begun by the former Prime Minister Yevgeny Primakov and designed to show that, from the *Cheka* to the KGB, Soviet foreign intelligence 'honourably and unselfishly did its patriotic duty to Motherland and people'. Andrew and Mitrokhin add the comment: 'Much as Russian intelligence has evolved since the collapse of the Soviet Union, it has yet to come to terms with its own past.'

> 'Much as Russian intelligence has evolved since the collapse of the Soviet Union, it has yet to come to terms with its own past.'
>
> —*The Mitrokhin Archive*

WHERE THE KGB SURVIVES

When the KGB was officially dissolved in December 1991, a few weeks before the Soviet Union itself, many international observers saw the arrival of the FSB as a possible sign that democracy would prevail in the newly-created Russian Federation. That assumption proved optimistic. In a volatile political environment, President Yeltsin and his advisors had to rely on state security and internal police for support.

On his home ground, Yeltsin was cautious in detailing his plans for the security services, beyond assurances that they would be very different from the KGB. What emerged was a structure for the climate of a new age: counter-terrorism gained a higher priority than counter-espionage. That meant closer liaison between the intelligence services of East and West – anathema only a decade before. A striking example is provided by *The Mitrokhin Archive,* which reveals that in 2004 at the holiday resort of Sochi on the Black Sea the FSB hosted a gathering of intelligence chiefs from 70 foreign services. That included senior representatives of Western agencies, all with the aim of discussing international collaboration in counter-terrorism. Ideologies were set aside: the explosive legacy of the 11 September 2001 terrorist outrage in the United States had ushered in a new age.

Solely in Belarus, landlocked republic in eastern Europe, the KGB lives on. Branded Europe's last dictatorship, Belarus has experienced an ongoing saga of struggle. Nazi occupation between 1941 and 1944 led to 2.2 million deaths. In 1945 a large part of western Belarus, formerly belonging to Poland, merged into the Soviet Union. During the 1960s, the Soviets implemented a 'Russification' process, curtailing use of the Belorussian language and culture.

Following independence and the start in 1994 of his presidency, Alexander Lukashenko (b. 1954) tightened the levers of power. Outlining the prevailing mood, he has proclaimed: 'No matter how hard the political demagogues have been trying to cross out the Soviet past from our history, the nation has prevented it.' The occasion of his pronouncement was significant. It was a ceremony to mark the reopening of a memorial complex in Minsk, prominent with a bust of former local boy Felix Dzerzhinsky.

The legislative branch of the Belarus government, the Supreme Soviet, thrives as a tribute to the old Soviet Union. Power rests constitutionally in the hands of the Council of Ministers. In practice, though, it is beholden to the Belarus Committee for State Security (KGB), which reports to the Council of Ministers as well as to the Supreme Soviet. When it comes to suppressing public dissent, KGB power is exercised through the *Almaz* (Anti Terrorist Unit), a tough, fully-armed cadre. During the 2006 presidential election campaign, known dissenters were warned that they faced the death penalty if they took part in protests which were defined by KGB chief Stepan Sukhorenko as 'terrorism' and therefore within the orbit of *Almaz*. Western reporters covering the election recorded that security agents gave no warning before opening fire on cars. Another prevailing fear was that critics would face the same fate as Dmitry Zavadskaya, a prominent critic of Lukashenko, who along with other crtitics, have 'disappeared'.

Today, Putin's Russia is desperate to stop a former Soviet state turning its back on Moscow and integrating with the EU and NATO. President George W. Bush has branded Belarus 'an outpost of tyranny' while allocating US$12 million dollars to promote democracy there. Meanwhile, the European Union funds pro-opposition radio broadcasts into Belarus as well as channeling money to pro-democracy groups. The overall aim may be regime change but, with all the muscle of the KGB, Lukashenko stands firm.

GLOSSARY

The functions of the security service operating in the Soviet Union remained broadly unchanged throughout its lifetime, although departments, weighed down by bureaucracy and individual rivalries, went through often confusing changes of name and structure. The familiar term 'KGB' is often used as a convenient shorthand to describe the entire intelligence apparatus, although strictly speaking, it dates from 1954 until the close of the Soviet Union.

Bolsheviks. From the Russian *Bolsheviki* ('majority faction'), these were breakaway members of the Marxist Russian Social Democratic Labour Party. Led by Lenin, they seized power in 1917 during the October Revolution.

Boyars. The cream of Russian land-owning nobility from the tenth to the seventeenth century, occupying the highest offices of state. They survived until the reign of Peter I ('the Great'), by which time their power had been progressively eroded. Their ranks and titles were finally abolished by Peter I.

Cheka. *Vserossiiskaya Chrezvychainaya Komissiya po Borbe s Kontr Revolyutsiyei i Sabotazhem* (Extraordinary Commission for Combating Counter Revolution and Sabotage). Existing from 1917–1922, the Cheka embodied three-man courts – *troikas* – with the power to investigate, arrest, prosecute and give out sentences.

Commissar. An official of the Communist Party in charge of political indoctrination and the enforcement of loyalty to the party.

FSB. *Federalnaya Sluzhba Bezopasnosti Rossiykoy Federatsii* (Federal Security Services of the Russian Federation). Possessing powers of detention and search, the successor to the KGB was created in 1995.

GKO. *Gosudarstvennyy Komitet Obrony* (Soviet State Committee for Defence). Under Beria, the committee oversaw all aspects of atomic bomb development.

GLAVLIT. *Glavnoe Upravlenie Po Delam Literatury I Izdatv* (Chief Administration for Safeguarding State Secrets in Print). The official print censorship organ of the Soviet Union was first formed in 1940. The title survived until the late 1980s. A similar organization exists within the Russian Federation today, entitled 'Main Administration For Safeguarding State Secrets in the Press'.

GPU. *Gosudarstvennoye Politicheskoye Upravleniye* (The State Political Administration). Created after the disbandment of the *Cheka*, the GPU was the secret police tasked to enforce state security. In 1934 it become incorporated into the NKVD.

GRU. *Glavnoye Razvedovatel'noye Upravlenie* (Main Intelligence Directorate). Created in 1918 by Lenin to handle all military intelligence from residencies, the GRU was totally independent of other Soviet power centres.

GULAG. *Glavnoye Upravlenie Lagerei* (Main Camp Administration). Originally signifying administration of the labour camps, the term was later broadened to include the entire system of Soviet slave labour.

KI. *Komitet Informatsii* (Information Committee). The Soviet foreign intelligence agency from 1947 to 1951, it had responsibility for domestic and military security.

KGB. *Komitet Gosudarstvennoy Bezopastni* (Soviet Security and Intelligence Service). From 1954 until November 1991, the KGB controlled organizations responsible for security, intelligence and the secret police. Following Beria's execution, it assumed all main internal and external security functions.

Kulaks. The term referred originally to relatively wealthy peasants who had prospered following the abolition of serfdom in Tsarist Russia. Under Soviet rule, kulaks were designated 'class enemies' and persecuted through Stalin's collectivization program.

MGB. *Ministerstvo Gosudarstvennoi Bezopastnosti* (Soviet Ministry of State Security). From 1946 to 1954, one of the many titles given to the Ministry for State Security.

MVD. *Ministerstvo Vnutrennikh Del* (Ministry of Internal Affairs). This title was used in Imperial Russia and later in the Soviet Union. Moscow based, it is still designated MVD in the Russian Federation.

NKGB. *Narodnyi Kommissariat Gozudarstvennoi Bezopastnosti* (People's Commissariat for State Security). Created in 1941, this was a police and counter intelligence force that in 1946 became the MGB.

NKVD. *Narodnyi Kommissariat Vnutrennikh Del* (People's Commisariat for Internal Affairs). Introduced in 1934 to succeed the OGPU, the NKVD were instrumental in Stalin's ethnic cleansing and genocide programmes. The NKVD had its own military units and held authority over the GULAG. In 1946 it was renamed the MVD and most of its responsibilities were passed to the MGB.

OGPU. *Obyedinennoye Gosudarstvennoye Politicheskoye Upravleniye* (Joint State Political Administration, also known as the All Union State Political Board). Created in 1922, it became the main agency responsible for internal security. The OGPU was incorporated into the NKVD in July 1934.

Okhrana. The Tsarist secret police from 1881 to 1917. As well as ensuring the safety of the Tsar and the Imperial family, it was responsible for internal security and combating attempts by Russian workers to form trades unions. Later functions included fighting terrorists and suspected revolutionaries.

Oprichniki. Members of a highly repressive private army of terror in the service of Tsar Ivan IV ('the Terrible'). *Oprichniki* were servants of the *Oprichnina* – derived from *Oprich*, meaning 'separate' or 'apart' – a state within a state serving the Tsar.

Politburo. *Politicheskoye Buro* (Political Bureau). The centre of power in the Soviet Union, this select group functioned as the central policy-making and governing body of the country. In 1919, the first Politburo consisted of five members: Lenin, Leon Trotsky, Joseph Stalin, Lev Kamenev and Nikolai Krestinsky.

Red Army. *Raboche-Krest'yanskaya Krasnanaya Armiya* (RKKA). Its full title was Workers' and Peasants' Red Army and it owned its origins to the 1918 Russian civil war. 'Red' denoted the blood shed by the working class. A political commissar was assigned to every unit who was authorized to override unit commanders' decisions if they clashed with Party principles.

SMERSH. *Smert Shpionam* ('Death to Spies'). Originally designated the 'Special Section', Stalin considered this name too mild and invented the title SMERSH. Formed during World War II, one of its main functions was following up the rear of the Red Army, arresting 'traitors, deserters, spies and criminal elements'.

Stasi. *Ministerium fur Staatssicherheit* (Ministry of State Security). The East German secret police had extensive programmes for internal repressions, international espionage, terrorism and terrorist training.

Streltsy. Meaning 'shooters', these were heavily armed units of Russian guardsmen, dating from the 1540s, who in Moscow protected the Tsar and the Kremlin.

BIBLIOGRAPHY

ANDREW, CHRISTOPHER AND OLEG GORDIEVSKY. *KGB: the Inside Story of its Foreign Operations from Lenin to Gorbachev.* London: Hodder & Stoughton, 1990.

ANDREW, CHRISTOPHER AND VASILI MITROKHIN. *The Mitrokhin Archive: The KGB in Europe and the West.* London: Penguin, 2000.

ANDREW, CHRISTOPHER. *The Mitrokhin Archive II: The KGB and the World.* London: Allen Lane, 2005.

ANDREYEV, CATHERINE. *Vlasov and the Russian Liberation Movement.* Cambridge: Cambridge University Press, 1987.

BRENT, JONATHAN AND VLADIMIR NAUMOV. *Stalin's Last Crime: The Plot against the Jewish Doctors.* London: John Murray, 2003.

CRANKSHAW, EDWARD. *Khruschev.* London: Collins, 1966.

COHEN, STEPHEN E. *Bukharin and the Bolshevik Revolution: A Political Biography, 1888–1938.* Oxford: Oxford University Press, 1991.

CONQUEST, ROBERT. *The Great Terror.* London: Macmillan, 1973.

CONQUEST, ROBERT. *The Nation Killers.* London: Macmillan, 1970.

DEAKIN, F.W. AND G.R. STORRY. *The Case of Richard Sorge.* London: Chatto &Windus, 1966.

DEVERE-SUMMERS, ANTHONY. *War and The Royal Houses of Europe.* London: Weidenfeld & Nicholson, 1997.

KEEP, JOHN L.H. *A History of the Soviet Union 1945–1991: Last of the Empires.* Oxford: Oxford Paperbacks, 2002.

LEVYTSKY, BORIS. *The Uses of Terror: The Soviet Secret Police 1917–1970.* London: Sidgwick and Jackson, 1972.

OVERY, RICHARD. *The Dictators: Hitler's Germany, Stalin's Russia.* London: Allen Lane, 2004.

PAGE, BRUCE, DAVID LEITCH, PHILLIP KNIGHTLEY. *Philby: The Spy Who Betrayed a Generation.* London: Andre Deutsch, 1968.

PAYNE, ROBERT. *The Life and Death of Lenin.* London: Harper Collins, 1987.

PHILBY, KIM. *My Silent War.* London: Arrow, 2003.

RAYFIELD, DONALD. *Stalin and His Hangmen: An Authoritative Portrait of a Tyrant and Those Who Served Him.* New York: Viking, 2004.

SEBAG-MONTEFIORE, SIMON. *Stalin: The Court of the Red Tsar.* London: Weidenfeld & Nicholson, 2003.

SERVICE, ROBERT. *Stalin: A Biography.* London: Pan Books, 2005.

SIMKIN, JOHN. *Stalin.* London: Spartacus Educational, Chrysalis Books, 1987.

STAFFORD, DAVID. *Spies Beneath Berlin.* London: John Murray, 2002.

TROYAT, HENRI. *Ivan The Terrible.* London: Weidenfeld & Nicholson, 2001.

WRIGHT, PETER. *Spy Catcher: The Candid Autobiography of a Senior Intelligence Officer.* London: Penguin Books, 1987.

INDEX

Page numbers in *italics* refer to photographs.

PICTURE CREDITS

Amber Books: 100, 101

Art-Tech/Aerospace: 26, 33, 40, 54, 76

Corbis: 6, 21, 22, 28, 31, 36, 38, 47, 48, 60, 63, 65, 70/71, 75, 90, 92, 98, 115, 116, 124, 127, 131, 133, 134, 148, 149, 151, 154, 157, 158, 159, 160, 163, 167, 171, 174, 181, 183

Mary Evans Picture Library: 17, 29, 139

Getty Images: 19, 34, 51, 57, 68, 74, 84, 91, 106, 121, 128, 132, 145, 146, 164, 165, 170, 178

Heritage Image Partnership: 10

David King Collection: 64, 67, 82, 96, 102

RIA Novosti Photo Library: 56, 113

Photos 12: 8

Popperfoto: 12, 78

TopFoto: Endpapers, 14, 23, 42, 44, 46, 53, 77, 80, 86, 110, 118, 130, 137, 140, 141, 142, 153, 173, 176

TRH Pictures: 87, 105

Ukrainian State Archive: 95, 104, 108, 109, 122